Ten Heritage Walks of
MUMBAI

Ten Heritage Walks of

MUMBAI

～ **Fiona Fernandez** ～

Photographs by
Disha art

Rupa & Co

Copyright © Fiona Fernandez 2007

Published 2007 by
Rupa & Co
7/16, Ansari Road, Daryaganj
New Delhi 110 002

Sales Centres:
Allahabad Bangalooru Chandigarh Chennai
Hyderabad Jaipur Kathmandu
Kolkata Mumbai Pune

Designed & typeset by
Mahendra M Kulkarni
Mumbai

Printed in India by
Nutech Photolithographers, New Delhi 110020

Contents

Introduction

he love affair began almost a decade ago - while being given charge of preparing a Mumbai-centric quiz. Being part of the college quiz club and tired of using rehashed questions from yearbooks and newspapers, I decided to attempt venturing into the holy sanctum for book lovers - the Asiatic Society Library (presently, one of my favourite hangouts!). As much as I was delighted to stumble on this sleeping giant of a library, the place overwhelmed me. I was submerged in a sea of information, thanks to the countless books on Mumbai that I could lay my hands on…the quiz was forgotten!

Over the years, the visits increased. Curiosity got the better of me. Leafing through so many invaluable publications about this city, I realised how truly blessed we are to be living in this marvel of a city and its unimaginable treasures: magnificent buildings, monuments, roads and structures, most of which are desperately trying to retain their age-old dignified identity. With time, the very same streets and lanes that were walked on, the buildings that went unnoticed - they all meant so much more. For each had a history behind it, an amusing tale to share or a juicy anecdote to chuckle on. And above all, each was a testimony of the city's wonderful past, that survived for centuries together.

This book is an ode to Mumbai, an honest and unpretentious attempt at rediscovering the city and its heritage. Like a faceless friend to the reader - be it the twenty-something city-bred Mumbaiite in search of that extra bit of trivia, or a curious tourist, the book takes you on ten fascinating and intriguing walks along the contours and corners that shaped this city. Marvel at Mumbai's glorious landmarks or its splendid mix of architecture, walk down its first roads, trace the roots of its vibrant cosmopolitan culture and ethnic fabric or simply soak in its grandiose history. What you will also find here are oft-forgotten, hidden nooks and distinct sights: intrinsic to the city in their own way.

Lose yourself among the narrow, congested bylanes of Bazaar Gate, marvel at the Gothic and Indo-Saracenic architecture within the Fort precinct or gaze at the Victorian ensemble of buildings as the afternoon sky blazes down on you from the city's expansive Oval Maidan. The rustic, earthy ambience of Dhobi Talao and Girgaum will transport you to a different Mumbai. It's all about small-time cloth merchants and sweetmeat marts, of Irani cafes and second-hand bookshops - reminiscent of a simpler time when Mumbai was Bombay and where horse-carriages at the Gateway were named after a British monarch!

These walks are largely spread across south and central Mumbai through Fort, Ballard Estate, Colaba and the inner parts of the city due to its high concentration of heritage structures and sights that comprise some of the oldest parts of the city. Bandra finds its way in this book by virtue of its charming past and its ties with the Portuguese since the fifteenth century.

While the book should not be regarded as a reference for the architectural and heritage sites of the city, it should be seen as an honest attempt in its own little way, a reminder from a die-hard Mumbaiite to value the city's treasures and how we should stop taking these for granted. After all, amidst the big 'C' called Commercialisation, it is us, the current generation, who can strive to revive it.

So here's an open invite that takes you for more than just a walk down memory lane....

ಬಃಲ

Acknowledgements

his book is for you, mom! From being my biggest support system to the most vocal critic and above all, for playing the anchor throughout this challenging and exciting phase as a writer - A big thank you!

I simply cannot proceed any further without mentioning Rupa & Co. for keeping faith in my writing this book, and for taking so much interest during the entire period.

My designer Mahendra, for doing full justice to the content and accurately conveying the mood of this book ever so splendidly. Not forgetting, the late hours, working through your Sundays and holidays - the end result says it all. The photography, courtesy Disha Art, truly captures Mumbai in all its grandeur and colour - apart from ceaselessly toying with my suggestions (and the weather too!) and Mahendra, for giving life to this book by ensuring that the unparalleled vibrancy and flavour of the city was never lost. This effort would have been incomplete without the continuous support of the Asiatic Society of Mumbai's ever-helpful and patient staff, particularly the Librarian, Maya Avasia, who took time out in between her hectic schedule to help me find my way through the gigantic maze of books and archives. Lensman Shirish Karale and 'Better Photography' also need to be thanked for sharing some wonderful photographs that have graced this book.

Our faithful taxi driver, Sandeep Kumar Dubey, should get an endurance award for patiently playing along with all our insane plans during the photo shoots; negotiating some of the worst roads, narrow bylanes and gullies and above all, keeping a cool head.

My friends and soulmates - Preeti, Sowmya, Sonali, Sudipta, ... all of you, in your own small way have been instrumental in imbibing a little bit of Mumbai in me - that inadvertently weaves its way in the book. Thanks for backing me one hundred per cent. And finally - for want of a better acknowledgement to my dear city, which has and will always inspire me - 'You can take a person out of Mumbai, but you cannot take Mumbai out of a person.'

Salaam Mumbai!

ಇಂಡ್

Getting Around

or a first-timer to the city who's interested in embarking on one of these walks, transport shouldn't really be a problem. Most walks start from important landmarks that can be reached by the public transport system. In case you are based in the suburbs, the best way to reach south Mumbai (for all walks except Walk 10) would be to commute via the local train. Safe, convenient and economical, they are the fastest means of getting around in Mumbai, and in context of this book, the easiest way to reach the starting points of most walks. The two main lines on which these trains run are Western Railway (terminating at Churchgate) and Central Railway (terminating at Chhatrapati Shivaji/Victoria Terminus). Just above the exit door of most local trains is a detailed map of the route it runs to guide the commuter. Fellow commuters can also be quite helpful. A note of caution here—avoid the morning rush which eases up post 10.30 am (both via road and rail) if you are headed towards south Mumbai.

Once you get off at the terminus, reaching the starting points should be easy, either via the BEST bus or a taxi or, in some cases, even on foot. The BEST bus service plies throughout the city and its suburbs and most bus stops along the route provide information concerning the stops it makes along the way. BEST depots are also helpful to the newcomer. Taxis in the city always run by the meter, so you can demand a meter card from your taxi driver when you have to pay for your ride and aren't sure about the rates. It's important that newcomers to the city are aware of this card; likewise, you even have a separate meter card while commuting in an autorickshaw. For Walk 10, which covers Bandra, you can travel in autorickshaws to get around - it is the only walk in this book that is sourced in the suburbs. First timers to the city should note that autorickshaws do not ply within city limits and are available only from Sion (Central line) and Bandra (Western line).

ॐ

The Weather Factor

*O*f course, when you do set out on these walks, take note of the all-important weather factor. The ideal time to experience these walks would be between November to February, as that's when Mumbai's weather gods are most accommodating! If you're still willing to brave the elements in summer months (March-May), then don't forget to equip yourself with a pair of sunglasses, a cap or headscarf, and some bottled water to beat the heat. Late afternoons would be the best time to venture out. And if you're one of those adventurous souls, happy to revel in the luxuriant whiff of the wet earth during Mumbai's (in)famous monsoon (June-September), then a raincoat should be your ideal companion. And forget about those dainty, foldable umbrellas - they should be reserved for your idyllic walks in the summertime!

Treasure Hunt Time: The Marvels of the Fort Precinct

(General Post Office - The Mint House - St. Thomas Cathedral)

*W*elcome to Mumbai's bustling commercial heartland - the Fort precinct. Actually, stop right there. This area may reflect the chaos of Mumbai - bumper-to-bumper traffic, countless office establishments jostling for space, hurried and hassled white-collared executives rushing to earn their moolah. Yet look closer, take a few minutes to absorb the surroundings. Amidst the concrete landscape are neoclassical, Gothic and Indo-Saracenic buildings, beautiful memorials and monuments, towering spires and a hidden past that tells a story. A story about a city that grew from a humble fishing village to a teeming megalopolis. Few areas in the city document its glorious past to such an extent as this part does. Marvel at the magnificent dome inside the General Post Office, stroll past the tree-lined avenues within the standardised business district of Ballard Estate, leaf through ancient manuscripts within the hallowed confines of the Asiatic Society Library at the Town Hall or simply bask in the breathtaking architecture of St. Thomas Cathedral and the Italian-styled façade of the Horniman Circle buildings. All this and more is for the taking. Walk on...

APPROXIMATE DISTANCE
2.5 kilometres

APPROACH/PARKING
Parking space comes at a premium in these parts of Mumbai's Fort area. Consider yourself lucky if you do manage to get parking outside the General Post Office or its whereabouts. The area is teeming with offices and business establishments and is highly congested, with most roads catering to public

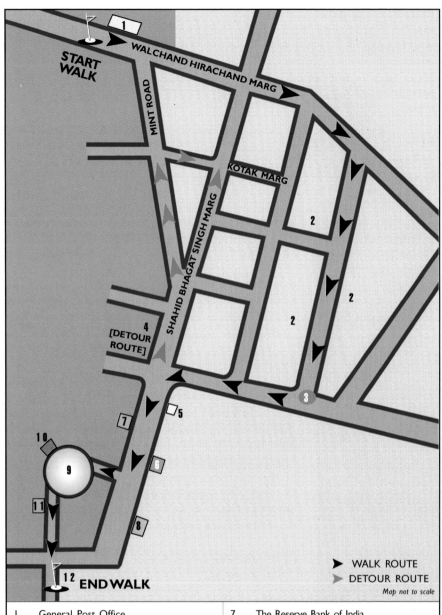

START
WALK

1

WALCHAND HIRACHAND MARG

MINT ROAD

KOTAK MARG

SHAHID BHAGAT SINGH MARG

2

2

2

4
[DETOUR
ROUTE]

3

5

7

6

10

9

8

11

12 END WALK

WALK ROUTE
DETOUR ROUTE
Map not to scale

1. General Post Office	7. The Reserve Bank of India
2. Ballard Estate	– original structure
3. Port Trust Memorial	8. The Asiatic Society of Mumbai
4. Way to Bazaar Gate Area	9. Horniman Circle Garden
5. The Mint House	10. Bombay Samachar Building
6. Bombay Castle and	11. St. Thomas Cathedral
INS Angre	12. Jimmy Boy Cafe

2

transport like the BEST buses, the yellow-and-black cabs or private vehicles. The ideal way to approach this route would be to hop on to a local train and reach the Chhatrapati Shivaji Terminus from where the starting point for this walk, i.e. the General Post Office, is barely a minute away.

PLACES OF INTEREST

- ❖ General Post Office
- ❖ Ballard Estate sub-precinct: Port, Port Trust Offices, Customs House, Kaiser-e-Hind building, Construction House
- ❖ Port Trust Memorial
- ❖ **DETOUR:** Bazaar Gate, Mint Road, Shahid Bhagat Singh Marg and its bylanes
- ❖ The Mint House
- ❖ Bombay Castle
- ❖ INS Angre
- ❖ The Reserve Bank of India - original structure
- ❖ The Town Hall housing the Asiatic Society of Mumbai
- ❖ Horniman Circle Garden
- ❖ Buildings around Horniman Circle with uniform building designs - State Bank of India, Indian Overseas Bank, Dena Bank and Zoroastrian Association buildings.
- ❖ Bombay Samachar newspaper office
- ❖ St. Thomas Cathedral
- ❖ Jimmy Boy Café off Bank Street

THE WALK

The immediate impression of the area is commotion and organised chaos. The unmistakable clockwork precision that the city is known for is most visible in these parts. This hub of commercial activity occupied a pivotal position, for it is around this epicentre that the origins of the city are found. As soon as one steps out of the western exit of the Chhatrapati Shivaji Terminus, the imposing General Post Office grabs one's attention.

CULINARY MUSINGS

The Light of Asia restaurant near the Devdas Purshottamdas Kothari Kabutarkhana and Pyaav (public water tank) opposite the General Post Office continues to dish out gastronomical delights to its faithful patrons, as it has done for over forty years now. Old-timers fondly recall the days when one could walk into this restaurant at an unearthly hour and be served with riotously hot Mutton Masala for a paltry sixty paise and chai for four annas, as strains of Ghulam Ali's melodious ghazals filled the restaurant.

Another old time favourite that has survived is the nearly half-a-century-old **City Kitchen**, tucked in the crowded Bazaar Gate area. Started by former India hockey goalkeeper Sacru Menezes, this eatery specialises in Goan homemade delights. It is a must-stop for Pork Vindaloo, Pork Sorpotel, Prawn Balchao, Bebinca and Goan Fish Curry, and for those who are adventurous and would try anything new on the menu—Stuffed Pigling!

General Post Office

It is to architect John Begg, that one must credit the Indo-Saracenic design of the General Post Office. Begg came to India in 1901, as Consulting Architect to Bombay (now Mumbai). In 1906, he was appointed Consulting Architect to the Government of India. Begg and fellow architect George Wittet were responsible for establishing the Indo-Saracenic style as the official style of architecture in British India. Considered Begg's most well-known design, the General Post Office was completed on 31 March 1913 at a total cost of Rs. 10,09,000.

The Central Dome of this structure bears a resemblance to Bijapur's Gol Gumbaz. Its vast Central Hall rises through the height of the building to the dome. It was built of local basalt with dressings of yellow stone from Kurla and white stone from Dhrangadhra. Spires with bearings of Moorish-styled architecture leave a lasting impression.

A Roll of Honour dedicated to members of the 'Post Office of India' who laid down their lives during World War I, situated near the main door, is easily overlooked. With forty-eight counters catering to daily transactions and some twenty or more for related mailing operations all over India and abroad, it justifies its title as - 'India's Busiest Post Office.' Postal employees carry on with

◄ *The magnificent Central Dome of the General Post Office, bearing a similarity with Bijapur's Gol Gumbaz*

The GPO is one of the city's finest examples of Indo-Saracenic architecture
▼

> **Named after General JH Ballard, who was the first Chairman of the Bombay Port Trust, this Estate was considered the most valuable and biggest holding of the Bombay (now Mumbai) Port Trust**

their work unperturbed by the historic air of the building.

Ballard Estate

Walk down from St. George's Road towards Walchand Hirachand Marg (formerly Wittet Road) to enter the Ballard Estate sub-precinct. The presence of the sea is unseen on its eastern edge as most buildings here belong to the Indian Navy and Mumbai Port Trust and are guarded behind high walls, presumably for security reasons.

This was the first consciously-planned sub-precinct in the city. Named after General JH Ballard, who was the first Chairman of the Bombay Port Trust, this Estate was considered the most valuable and biggest holding of the Bombay (now Mumbai) Port Trust. The area was developed to decongest the already bustling office space in the Fort locality. It was converted from a sea-flooded foreshore that was extracted as a result of the spoils obtained from constructing the Alexandria Dock, into one of the most prestigious official addresses in the city. Spread over twenty-two acres, it was laid out by Consulting Architect of the Bombay Port Trust, George Wittet in

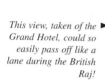

The Grand Hotel is a striking landmark as one enters Ballard Estate, known for its prominent location in this business district ◄

This view, taken of the ► Grand Hotel, could so easily pass off like a lane during the British Raj!

the European Renaissance style of architecture between 1908-14. It was primarily built as a premium business district, with forty-three blocks of neat office buildings with broad, well-kept thoroughfares, comparable to the very best in the British Empire at that time.

Today, Ballard Estate remains one of the premier office addresses of Mumbai. Some interesting stopovers within the Estate could be at the Grand Hotel, that occupies a large corner site in the Estate. Opened in 1922, it was situated near the Ballard Pier and offered a variety of dining and other facilities to its ship-weary passengers. In the 1920s and 30s, the Grand was the most sought-after deluxe hotel in the city and was the preferred choice of stay, especially among European visitors.

On Sri Sivasagar Ramgulam Marg (formerly Sprott Road), past Grand Hotel, one sees rows of neoclassical style buildings. The Construction House (at the junction of the Wittet and Nicol Roads) built in the 1930s was one of the earliest buildings to be fully air-conditioned in the area. Several buildings that came up in that period bear a similar architectural style, like the magnificent construction currently known as Reliance House, the Scindia Steam Navigation building, the *Kaiser-e-Hind* Building, the Exchange Building (that houses the Office of the Deputy Salt Commissioner) and the offices of the Post Master General for Foreign Mails.

The Vakils House, Northern Marine House and the neogothic building that house

Some of the details of the ◄ architecture on the buildings in Ballard Estate. Most of these are commercial premises and have retained their distinct character, thankfully

◄ Another renovated and
well maintained
commercial building in
Ballard Estate

the motion picture giants - Paramount and Universal Pictures - are some of the constructions whose design, architecture and façades are in pristine condition. Quaint cafés like the Model Restaurant and the New Hindu Hotel still stand, albeit not for too long, not surprising amidst the fury and frenzy with which the concrete revolution threatens to take over the area. Another quaint, cozy restaurant is the Britannica & Co 'High Class Restaurant' in Wakefield building. Packed tables cater to tourists and office-goers, the whiff of fish and chips pervading the smoke-filled air of this recently revived café. The impressive, slightly run-down Indo-Saracenic building is believed to have been designed by the architect Wittet. Its namesake - a trendier, modern version, called Café Britannia - can be seen on the adjacent R. Kamani Marg.

The Estate is still home to the impressive New Customs House and its offices that cover a huge portion on the southern end of the Estate opposite the Mint House. George Wittet has designed this building as well. Other offices that have more or less disappeared from the area belonged to the British India Steam Navigation, Burmah-Shell Oil Storage and Distribution Company, His Majesty's Trade Commissioner's office and numerous shipping, banking and insurance firms. In fact, the British India Steam Navigation building was the last to be designed by noted city-architect FW Stevens on R. Kamani Marg.

Opposite the New Customs House, where Ramgulam Marg ends and meets Shoorji

The Bombay Port Trust insignia that can be sighted on the Memorial

◄ *Winged lions carved at the base of the Port Trust Memorial*

DID YOU KNOW?

On January 1, 1915, a new **Port Trust Railway** was established, that ran parallel to the city's port, docks and natural harbour and connected Ballard Pier with Wadala. The Ballard Pier became the point of arrival for foreign ships and its railway terminal nearby connected passengers entering the Indian sub-continent by rail via the Victoria Terminus. In fact, on scheduled mail steamer days, the Ballard Pier railway terminus was abuzz with activity, plying special trains to and from Calcutta, Peshawar and Delhi.

Vallabhdas Road (formerly Ballard Road), is the bronze and gilt-edged Port Trust War Memorial, erected by the Bombay Port Trust. With the Dorabshaw Building in the background, this memorial is another structure that came up in the early half of the twentieth century. A closer look at this almost-forgotten memorial and one learns of the invaluable support provided by the Port Trust for the greater cause of World War I. The first transport for the War left from the city's port on August 21, 1914. On the memorial, a plaque reads:

'1,87,000 troops embarked and disembarked from the Port...

3,046 transports and 668 hospital ships were dealt with at the docks...

A scene from the narrow, ▶
congested Bazaar Gate area

2,073 troop and hospital trains were railed over the Port Trust Railway...

494 Government ships used the Port Trust Dry Docks...

22,28,000 tons of military stores were shipped from the port.'

The Port Trust Administrative Offices are towards the southwest corner of the Estate. Nearby are the splendid offices belonging to Gresham Life Assurance, as well as the Headquarters of the Maharashtra Naval Area that came up in the 1930s. Both buildings stand at the junction where Shapoorji Road and Mint Road meet to join Shahid Bhagat Singh Marg.

DETOUR: Bazaar Gate area - Mint Road, Shahid Bhagat Singh Marg and its bylanes (Fort Market)

Explore the congested yet architecturally diverse older parts of the Fort by taking a detour after you complete the tour of Ballard Estate. Before proceeding towards the Mint House and the rest of the heritage buildings

along this walk, a short route can be covered within the Bazaar Gate area. The area is so called because of the old Bazaar Gate - one of the three gates built around the walls of the long-gone Fort. The gate no longer exists, yet this crowded and commercial locality retains its name. The city's British rulers referred to this area outside the Gate as the 'Black Town' or 'Native Town', as it housed the bulk of the middle and lower class Indian residents who built their dwellings and businesses around the fortifications. In complete contrast, the richer Indians, mostly merchants, lived within the high Fort walls.

Situated towards the northern portion of the original Fort, remnants of the original bazaar are still seen, as the architecture is more or less intact. Traders of all communities had their shops and establishments in the narrow, congested lanes. The building pattern reflected the diverse local styles of traditional Indian architecture. Most of today's Mint Road and its bylanes, like Agiary Lane, Kumta Street and Mangalore Street, still depict some of the chaos yet misty, old-world charm of a bygone era.

The natives who resided in the area were mainly Banias, Gujaratis and Bohri Muslims, who were encouraged by the East India Company to set up their trade in the burgeoning township. They brought along their own lifestyles and architecture and merged it with the landscape. A distinct pattern of long, narrow parallel streets mushroomed in the locality comprising of narrow buildings with teakwood framed interiors and exteriors. Extremely narrow and tall buildings with little or no space between each other were integral to the area.

With time, the architecture in this area improved and decorative façades, ornate teakwood balconies began to show up in building designs. Strong influences from

DID YOU KNOW?

The western edge of the highly uniform Ballard Estate, closer to the congested Bazaar Gate was a zone that was earlier occupied by piers along the sea front. As a result, when these areas were landfilled, these long strips of development came up with streets that were named after southwestern ports like **Goa Street, Mangalore Street and Cochin Street**. Separate piers catered for transport and trade for each of these ports. One can still walk down these nondescript and sleepy-looking bylanes and steal a glimpse of custom and trading houses - the few that have defied time.

Gujarati styles of domestic architecture, especially in the intricate woodwork, could be seen. A walk down these lanes and one can see a few of these surviving buildings jostling for elbow room amidst the newer, concrete multiple-storied constructions. This street and building pattern is in complete contrast to the elaborate design plans that highlighted the neoclassical and Gothic style of its more famous neighbours.

The Mint House

Standing close to the Town Hall is the Mint House. This plain yet dignified building with an Ionic portico, designed by Major J. Hawkins in the neoclassical style of architecture, dates back to 1829. The Mint House was the first construction to represent this early distinctive architectural style of British India. Being the earliest notable and prominent public building to be built within the Fort, it became the chosen mode of building designs by the East India Company in that period.

The Mint House was the first construction to represent this early distinctive architectural style of British India

The Mint House occupies an area of 60,000 square yards and was reclaimed from the sea in 1823. It is here that India's currency is coined. Permission to see the interiors of the Mint can be obtained from the Mint Master. The Reserve Bank of India building that came up nearly a century later beside the Mint House reinforced the area's importance as the financial nucleus of India.

Bombay Castle

Near the Mint House and behind the Town Hall, are the extremely interesting remains of the Bombay Castle. Now under the control of the Indian Navy, this structure was constructed by the earliest British settlers on the skeletal framework of wealthy botanist and early city resident Garcia D'Orta's palatial mansion, known then as the 'Manor House'. The area also houses the last surviving fortifications of the city's Fort walls. It was the lone existing structure overlooking the Bombay harbour for a long time that later became the starting point around which the first Portuguese, and later English settlements were built, giving rise to the town of Bombay. The House was partially destroyed by Arab marauders in 1661.

This Castle grew till the seventeenth century when Bombay was still confined to being a trading port township. It was only after the consolidation of trade in the early nineteenth century that public buildings came up in the vicinity of the Castle. The Castle was the original residence of Bombay's early governors and by the mid-nineteenth century the British built the second largest arsenal in India, here. It also housed a temporary chapel in the 1660s - until the St. Thomas Cathedral came up in the 1700s - in two rooms within the Castle, for the Protestant population that mainly comprised of troops in the Bombay Fort and the Company's servants.

Today, the old Manor House is absorbed into a new building with Naval offices and only a minor part of the original structure is visible. Special permission is needed to view the interiors of this high security zone.

INS Angre

Within the Bombay Castle complex are the Western Naval Command headquarters known as the INS Angre. Named after the famous Maratha sea admiral and shrewd

---

DID YOU KNOW?

According to a map drawn by Jacques de Funck in 1756, the **Bombay Castle and Fort** comprised of a Government House, Council Room, Stores Room and Treasury. This apart, it had a Flagstaff, Artillery Barracks, Infantry Officer's Guard Room, Barracks for Relieving Guard, different lodgments for Company servants, a water tank and a huge gate at the entrance of the Castle. The Castle stood at the lower part of the central portion that formed the Bombay Town.

The INS Angre has witnessed the port city's
history unfold over centuries together

warrior Kanhoji Angre, who won several sea
battles, it is part of the extended high security
zone belonging to the Indian Navy.

The INS Angre was formerly known as
the Bombay Castle Barracks and came up as
early as in 1548. The castle gateway has a
watchtower with three smaller towers that
stand against the backdrop of the ramparts of
the ruins of the Fort.

It was christened as a prominent Indian
naval establishment on 15 September 1951.
This large naval settlement houses twenty-five
old war guns, battlements, ancient sundials,
doorways and an impressive bas-relief entrance
gate. It was first commissioned as HMIS
Dalhousie on 25 July 1940. When India became
a republic on 26 January 1950, it was renamed
as INS Dalhousie. On 15 September 1951, it
became INS Angre. Today, it is a major logistics
base for the Western Naval Command. The
original gateway to the castle now forms the
main entrance to the naval establishment.

The Reserve Bank of India (original structure)

The need to establish a headquarter for the country's premier banking institution resulted in establishing the Reserve Bank of India in Mumbai to complement the Mint House in the vicinity. The bank was built on a plot at an angle formed by Mint Road and Bazaar Gate Street. JA Ritchie of the famous architectural firm Palmer & Turner was the chief architect.

This utilitarian structure was opened in April 1939. Giving a lasting impression of standardised design and solidity, it remains one of the finest examples of construction using Malad stone, found in the northern extensions of the city's boundaries at the time. Two giant stone columns on either side mark the entrance to this financial landmark.

The Reserve Bank of India was established on the recommendations of the Hilton Young Commission and the Bank

> Giving a lasting impression of standardised design and solidity, it remains one of the finest examples of construction using Malad stone, found in the northern extensions of the city's boundaries at the time

commenced operations on 1 April 1935 with Sir Osborne Smith as its first Governor. It took over the functions that were performed by the Controller of Currency and the Imperial Bank of India. Initially set up as a shareholder's bank, it was nationalised in 1949.

◄
The Reserve Bank of India is truly representative of the city's vibrant economic and financial supremacy

The symbol representing the Reserve Bank of India
▼

DID YOU KNOW?

Burma (now Myanmar) seceded from the Indian Union in 1937, yet the **Reserve Bank of India** continued to act as the Central Bank of Burma until the Japanese occupied Burma and finally gave up control of it in 1947. In fact, even after its partition from Pakistan, the Reserve Bank served as the Central Bank of Pakistan till June 1948.

In order to complement the working of the country's premier bank, a modern, commercial building housing additional offices of the Reserve Bank came up in the early 1980s. This whitewashed skyscraper reflects the contrasts in the styles of architecture that pervades the landscape of the Fort precinct.

The Town Hall, housing the Asiatic Society of Mumbai

Perhaps, no other institution in the city has such a glorious past as the Asiatic Society of Mumbai. This internationally acclaimed and renowned seat of learning was the brainchild of the then Recorder of Bombay, Sir James Mackintosh. He was the founder-president of the Asiatic Society and had a vision to establish a, 'suitable building for public meetings and entertainment and also make a home for the Library and Museum of the Literary Society....' The birth of the Society took place in 1804 at the Government House

◄ *The historic Town Hall of the Asiatic Society of Mumbai, facing the Horniman Circle Gardens, remains one of its most important centres of learning and progress; a landmark unparalleled*

in 'Parell' (today's Parel), where seventeen gentlemen including Governor Jonathon Duncan gathered to establish the Literary Society of Bombay.

Mackintosh reintroduced an earlier proposal to build a new Town Hall facing the open space opposite the Bombay Green. This site was initially turned down by the East India Company because they felt it would 'obstruct the military exercises' due to its proximity to the harbour and port. Thankfully, the decision was reversed in 1818 and the Society commissioned architect Colonel Thomas Cowper to design the magnificent Town Hall.

Work began in 1821. Along with Captain Charles Waddington, two architects from the Bombay Engineers completed this impressive city landmark in 1833 in its distinct neoclassical style at a cost of Rs. 65,669. Eight splendid Doric columns stand at the main pediment portico. Entirely built of Porbander stone, the upper level's hundred square feet houses the Grand Assembly Hall, (now converted to a public Reading Hall) that was earlier used for public meetings and balls. It boasted of a spectacular organ gifted by Sir Albert Sassoon as well as a movable stage capable of seating 250 performers. The elite Durbar Hall, is to the northeast of the entrance, exclusively meant for the Society's meetings since its inception. In 1827, the Society joined the Royal Asiatic Society of Great Britain and Northern Ireland as its Bombay branch. After 1947, it simplified its name to become the Asiatic Society of Bombay and finally in 1954, it democratised itself by adopting its current nomenclature.

The Asiatic Library, located within the Town Hall, was founded in 1804 by Mackintosh 'for the investigation and encouragement of Oriental arts and sciences.' It is home to over 2,000 Oriental manuscripts, a galaxy of rare matriculation examinations. In fact, the first batch of graduates from the University, including Mahadeo Govind Ranade and Ramakrishna Gopal Bhandarkar, gave their examinations in the Town Hall!

In 1920, the Asiatic Society assigned the Victoria and Albert Museum (now named after Bhau Daji Lad) as custodian of its treasures and thereby transferred to the Museum its entire collection of mineral specimens, archaeological artifacts and other rare treasures except for the coins and Buddhist relics, which it retains till today.

Horniman Circle

The Fort had within its area, a large open space in the centre known as the Bombay Green that was exactly behind the Bombay Castle. Governor Bartle Frere's first commissioned project was structuring the Bombay Green to the Elphinstone Circle. It was then named after Frere's predecessor, Governor Lord John Elphinstone. Frere laid the foundations for the Circle buildings in October 1864. It was a place of recreation for children and continued to be so even when the Elphinstone Circle

editions, over 1,00,000 volumes on literature, arts and social sciences, nearly 10,000 Indian coins and several editions of early Bombay newspapers and journals.

The Grand Assembly Room has life-like statues of Governor Montstuart Elphinstone, Governor John Malcolm, Governor Sir Bartle Frere, famous city and Society benefactor Sir Jagannath Shankarseth and India's first baronet Sir Jamshetji Jeejeebhoy within its hallowed interiors.

In the early years of the Bombay University, the Town Hall was the venue of the

Right/ Facing page: ►
Images taken from various angles to capture the uniform yet striking architecture found among the buildings and its arcades at the Horniman Circle

design of the Town Hall. The gardens were laid out in 1869 covering an area of 12,081 square yards and completed shortly before the Duke of Edinburgh's visit in 1872. An ornamental fountain still adorns the centre of the gardens. Today, the gardens often play host to street plays and theatre festivals in a bid to revive public interest for this historic landmark.

The arcade was designed to offer protection to pedestrians from the scorching sun as well as the torrential rain. Some of the notable establishments housed in the circle that still survive include the State Bank of India (1924) and those that sprung up later, like Dena Bank, Indian Overseas Bank and Zoroastrian Association Building. The unique, integrated precinct was built with Porbander stone facings and terracotta finials and keystones. In 1947, the Circle was renamed after B.G. Horniman - the renowned pro-freedom editor of the *Bombay Samachar* press English language daily *Bombay Chronicle*.

Gardens were erected. The first building that came up was the Bank of Bombay. Some of the other offices included Messrs. Remington & Co., Messrs. Nicol & Co., Branch Bank of Bengal, Accountant General's Office, Bombay Collector's and General Stamp Office, Chartered Bank of India and the Chartered Mercantile Bank.

This was a partly-sponsored smaller scale project that involved restructuring the wide open space into a formal, circular park enclosed by an assembly of architecturally unified commercial establishments. The design for this façade was meant to instill a sense of uniformity and it was the first time that such an urban unified design approach was adopted in India. It was structured as a classical circle that complemented the neoclassical

►
One of the architecturally impressive buildings near Horniman Circle

The Bombay Samachar building housing Asia's oldest daily newspaper, at Horniman Circle

Below: The famous white coloured water fountain in the courtyard of the St. Thomas Cathedral

Bombay Samachar and its legacy

Furdonjee Marzbanjee is often regarded as the father and founder of the native press in India. A respected printer and publisher, he set up the *Bombay Samachar* - a Gujarati language daily newspaper from his offices near the Horniman Circle Gardens. It was from this unique red-brick façade building

that the first edition was launched on 1 July 1822.

The newspaper is still in circulation and is today regarded as Asia's oldest surviving newspaper. Today, the area in the vicinity and the road on which this historic building and printing press stands, bears the name of this famous landmark - Bombay Samachar Marg. It was also the same concern that brought out the *Bombay Chronicle* - its English counterpart that hasn't survived, unlike its Gujarati cousin.

St. Thomas Cathedral

Except for its towering spire, this historic and beautiful place of worship which is opposite the entrance of the Horniman Circle Gardens is nearly lost among the hustle and bustle of its surroundings. It was the city's first Anglican church built by the earliest British settlers in order to provide them with church services. During Rev. Richard Cobbes, term as chaplain of Bombay (between 1714-21) funds amounting to Rs. 43,992 were raised for building a new church. Governor Gerald Aungier, authorised its construction way back in 1672 but work reached a standstill after the walls of the church were complete. Renewed attempts and fresh funds from wealthy British residents saw to it that the

Some of the outstanding memorials honour Colonel Burr, who commanded the Battle of Kirkee (1817), Captain GD Hardinge, who died in battle when the English captured the French cruiser Piemontaise (1808), and Colonel John Campell, defender of Mysore against Tipu Sultan in 1784, thus making the cathedral an unbelievable showcase of historic events. Aungier gifted one of the chalices to the cathedral in 1675 while another came from merchants of the city of York. Wealthy citizen and benefactor Sir Cowasjee Jehangir Readymoney erected the ornate fountain that faces the cathedral. Another spectacular addition was the organ case with ironwork designed by noted architect of the time, Thomas Roger Smith, in 1865.

construction was fully complete, nearly forty years later, when its doors were opened for services on Christmas Day in 1718.

The church still has splendid oyster-shell windows that allow only a misty, pearly, diffused light to enter its interiors. Such effort and detail was put into its construction that even its roof was cannonball-proof! The church underwent several transformations before it came to be the grand cathedral it is today. Initially, the flooring was made of earth, smeared with cow dung and had windowpanes of thin shells of mother-of-pearl. In 1816, it was consecrated in the name of St. Thomas, the Apostle of India and in 1838, it was designated the Cathedral Church of the See. The Gothic-styled clock and tower was added in 1838. It is a virtual museum, with memorials and monuments within its premises.

◀ *St. Thomas Cathedral, at Horniman Circle, was an important historic as well as religious structure to the British presence in the city*

Jimmy Boy Café

After a most enthralling walk down memory lane, you may give your feet a rest and treat yourself to some fabulous Parsi fare with a short hop across to the Jimmy Boy Café, tucked in a corner off Bank Street. This recently renovated Parsi restaurant is a hot favourite among office-goers in the vicinity. The Irani connection is natural because Jimmy Boy was originally an Irani restaurant called Café India for fifty-five years under proprietor Boman A. Irani. Aspi J. Irani, who took charge, worked wonders and transformed it into today's Jimmy Boy Café. The Parisian café-like ambience and old-world interiors coupled with its arched windows, impressive chandeliers and teakwood furniture make it the ideal stop for a relaxed lunch. Gorge on the lagan-nu-bhonu, patra ni machhi, jardaloo sali boti and chicken dhansak, but don't forget to leave sufficient room for the lip-smacking lagan-nu-custard. Without doubt, it makes perfect sense to end your walk here!

Into the Heart of the Fort: Beyond Flora Fountain & Kala Ghoda

(Standard Chartered Building - Rhythm House - Esplanade Mansion)

Mumbaiite would undoubtedly agree that all roads lead to Flora Fountain. This is as central in Mumbai city as one can get - be it from the Central or Western Railway terminuses, the harbour, or the commercial districts of Fort, Nariman Point or Ballard Estate. Flora Fountain and its surroundings—all the way up to the Kala Ghoda sub-precinct—is probably the shortest walk featured in the book. Yet, do not be fooled into thinking there is any paucity of historic and heritage sites. Within this barely one kilometre stretch are some of the biggest and oldest commercial and national banks, housed in impressive neogothic, Indo-Saracenic or Victorian buildings. Add to these magnificent structures some of the most important commercial establishments that have survived many decades, quaint restaurants, libraries, hotels and places of worship, which may have been lost among the pages of history. If that isn't enough heritage for your itinerary, then bring in the beautiful and culturally rich sub-precinct of Kala Ghoda that constitutes the second half of this walk.

APPROXIMATE DISTANCE
   1 kilometre

APPROACH/PARKING
   Flora Fountain is equidistant from both the Churchgate and Chhatrapati Shivaji Terminus railway stations. It barely takes you ten minutes to reach the starting point of this walk from either of these two terminuses. Alternatively, if you're taking the road, then parking at the Flora Fountain is quite an arduous

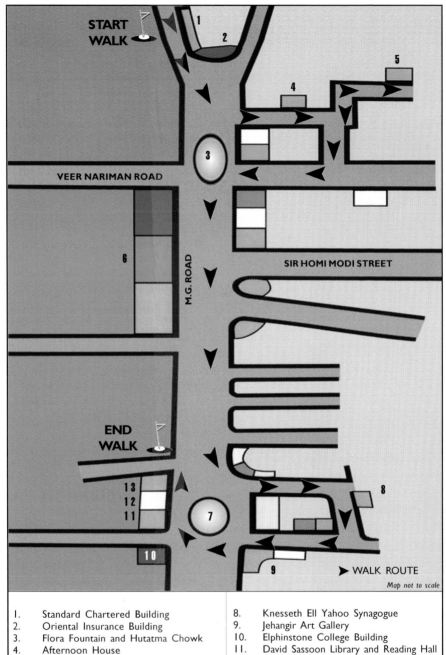

START WALK

VEER NARIMAN ROAD

M.G. ROAD

SIR HOMI MODI STREET

END WALK

1

2

3

4

5

6

7

8

9

10

11

12

13

► WALK ROUTE

Map not to scale

1.	Standard Chartered Building	8.	Knesseth Ell Yahoo Synagogue
2.	Oriental Insurance Building	9.	Jehangir Art Gallery
3.	Flora Fountain and Hutatma Chowk	10.	Elphinstone College Building
4.	Afternoon House	11.	David Sassoon Library and Reading Hall
5.	Banaji Limji Agiary	12.	Army and Navy Building
6.	HSBC, Bank of India and ANZ Grindlays	13.	Esplanade Mansion
7.	Kala Ghoda		

task. Being surrounded by commercial establishments from every side makes it doubly difficult. So, boarding any of the Colaba or Mantralaya-bound BEST buses from the Chhatrapati Shivaji Terminus wouldn't be a bad idea to reach Flora Fountain.

PLACES OF INTEREST

- ❖ Standard Chartered Building
- ❖ Oriental Insurance Buildings
- ❖ Flora Fountain & Hutatma Chowk
- ❖ Nanabhai Lane - Afternoon House
- ❖ Banaji Limji Agiary
- ❖ Akbarallys department store
- ❖ Pundole Art Gallery and surrounding commercial establishments around Flora Fountain square
- ❖ Central Bank Building
- ❖ Old Oriental Bank
- ❖ Bank offices - HSBC, Bank of India & ANZ Grindlays
- ❖ Lanes and buildings from State Bank of Hyderabad to Jehangir building on MG Road
- ❖ Khyber Restaurant
- ❖ Kapoor Lamp Shades
- ❖ Kala Ghoda
- ❖ Rhythm House
- ❖ Knesseth Ell Yahoo Synagogue
- ❖ Chetana Cultural Centre
- ❖ Oricon Building
- ❖ Max Mueller Bhavan on Rampart Row
- ❖ Jehangir Art Gallery
- ❖ Elphinstone College
- ❖ David Sassoon Library and Reading Room
- ❖ Army and Navy Building
- ❖ Esplanade Mansion

THE WALK

What strikes you about this walk is the unbelievably high number of impressive and equally important banks and commercial establishments within such a small radius. Many of them are more than 150 years old, with history written all over their walls and interiors. All through this walk you get the impression that the commercial is completely in sync with the historic character of these buildings. Its character, charm and link with the past is intact, thankfully. This walk begins at the Standard Chartered Building.

Standard Chartered Building

It represents the first of the banks along Mahatma Gandhi Road within this thriving Bank District. Originally called the Chartered Bank of India, Australia and China, it was one of Sir F.W. Stevens' last works. This recently renovated building stands out for its Porbander, Malad and basalt stone in light colours and traditional ceramic tiles for its roof - typical of the architecture in the area. Unfortunately, Stevens could not live to see this project complete, though he was fully involved with its work till his death on 5 March 1900.

The building was given the status of a Grade-II heritage structure for its neoclassical design and impeccable stonework carvings and façades. Gostling & Stevens designed the offices within the building in 1898. Its construction began a year later and the bank was eventually completed in December 1902 at the cost of Rs. 6,00,000. This bank assumed immense importance as it traded with the British colonies and contacts of the British Empire in its most prosperous era. Moreover, it was the most centralised location between London and the Far East. The premises consisted of a banking hall, offices, private apartments for the director and his family and even servants quarters - all of which was personally supervised by Stevens' son,

►

Standard Chartered Building

> ## This Gothic-styled building was strategically positioned opposite the Flora Fountain and the Central Telegraph Office

tapering of two important roads—the Mahatma Gandhi Road and Dr. DN Road, and was built in the form of a 'V'. F.W. Stevens was the immediate choice to remodel the building when it was to be converted to the Oriental Life Insurance Building. He added another level, as well as a steeply sloping roof. An interesting addition was a series of three sculptured portrait heads of the three founders of the Assurance Company that protrude from the building, below which are engraved the words 'Oriental Buildings'.

Today, it houses the American Express Bank and remains one of the best examples of a corner building design. It is also a Grade-I heritage site.

Flora Fountain and Hutatma Chowk

Flora Fountain was built on a spot that has been an anchor of sorts through the many transformations that Mumbai has witnessed over time. It was built at the heart of the Fort precinct to demarcate the junction of the bow-like cross axis that ran across the early city.

Built as a dedication to Governor Sir Bartle Frere (1862-67), it was even called the Frere Fountain initially, for a while. Frere was responsible for the vibrant and enterprising planning of the new town. It was designed by a committee that included R. Norman Shaw in Britain. The fountain was sculpted in fine imported stone from Portland by James Forsythe and eventually placed at the square in 1869. It was built to represent the Roman goddess of flowers - Flora - and is surrounded by a host of small fountains and mythological figurines.

Charles. The interior woodwork, counters and furniture were obtained from Messrs Alex Mackenzie & Co. of the Byculla Saw Mills. Its original grandeur is still visible.

This building was one of the first heritage buildings to be restored in Mumbai. It started a positive trend in the city among owners of heritage buildings, to conserve the city's surviving treasures.

Oriental Life Insurance Building

Interestingly, the site of this building was the former home of Cathedral High School. The construction of this new, imposing commercial building began in late 1895-early 1896 and ended in 1898, at a total cost of Rs. 4,50,000. The school wings (Junior and High) later moved to their present addresses. The Junior School stands nearby, while the Middle and Senior wings are situated near the JN Petit Girls' School on Maharshi Dadhichi Road.

This Gothic-styled building was strategically positioned opposite the Flora Fountain and the Central Telegraph Office. The original school building was designed much earlier, in 1878-85, and complemented the

Previous Page: Oriental Life Insurance Building

Flora Fountain, named after the ► Roman Goddess Flora

At the turn of the century, the Flora Fountain was enclosed by a circular garden. Today, it has become the centre of a huge parking lot surrounded by the nerve of the city's business establishments. Nearby is the Hutatma Chowk (Martyr's Square) that was built to commemorate the sacrifice of hundreds of freedom fighters who lost their lives in the struggle to ensure Maharashtra's statehood.

Afternoon House - Nanabhai Lane

The address is legendary among Mumbai's journalistic success stories - Afternoon House, 6 Nanabhai Lane. *The Afternoon Despatch & Courier* newspaper was the dream of one man who knew the city and wrote about it like no other - Behram Contractor a.k.a. Busybee. Until he passed away a couple of years ago, he remained an integral part of this newspaper. His striking wit was best visible in his daily column 'Round and About' that managed to sift out a deeper understanding of the pulse of this city.

He helped launch the *Afternoon* newspaper on 25 March 1985 and with it a new chapter was added to the city's pulsating fourth estate culture. The paper is eighteen years old, going on nineteen, and is housed in a splendid, quaint-looking ninety-year-old

The Afternoon House on Nanabhai Lane, home to the English-language daily The Afternoon Despatch & Courier

The Banaji Limji Agiary

Below: The Readymoney Mansion,
near Flora Fountain, retains a
distinctly Indian character with its
balcony design

building steeped in history. It is tucked away in one of the oldest parts of the early city, formed nearly two centuries ago. No doubt, the newspaper is a tribute to the genius of a man whose vision was simple, yet managed to touch the hearts of so many Mumbaiites.

Banaji Limji Agiary

Hidden from public gaze, in the narrow bylanes off Fountain is the almost-forgotten Banaji Limji Agiary on Agiary Street. An agiary is the place of worship for the Zoroastrian community, for whom worship of fire is integral to religious practice. What lies within the walls of this nondescript-looking exterior is the oldest sacred fire in the city, that arrived here on 25 June 1709 from Kolkata. Seth Banaji Limji, a wealthy merchant from Surat, endowed it. It was also called 'Kote-ni-agiary' (Fire Temple of the Fort). The agiary was severely damaged during the Great Fire that ravaged the Fort in 1805 and the sacred fire was temporarily transported to the Soonaji Hirji Readymoney Agiary at Gowalia Tank. It was installed in its new home on 15 April 1845 when it returned to the new building on Agiary Street, thanks to generous fund-raising from its community at the time. In fact, there was a time when this agiary was unique in housing the only seminary or madrassa in the city.

Akbarallys Department Store

Probably, the native Indian's answer to the swanky British departmental stores that sprung up all over the city in the late nineteenth and

> The gallery was established in 1963 by Kali Pundole, who began work as a framer, selling framed reproductions of paintings torn from pages of the *Illustrated Weekly of India*

early twentieth century, Akbarallys showed no prejudice whatsoever to non-Europeans. Over a 100 years old and still running, it still holds its own in the twenty-first century. This 'no-frills' department store opened to the public in 1897 and is housed next to the Readymoney Mansion at Veer Nariman Road near the Flora Fountain Square.

Ask any septuagenarian to name his or her favourite shopping address in the city and pat comes the reply in favour of this 'homely' department store that retains a faithful clientele.

Pundole Art Gallery and surrounding commercial establishments

One of the earliest art galleries to spring up in the heart of the city was the Pundole Art Gallery. The gallery was established in 1963 by Kali Pundole, who began work as a framer, selling framed reproductions of paintings torn from pages of the *Illustrated Weekly of India*. Flipping through its pages gave Pundole an insight into Indian art and its unsung artistes, and he was deeply inspired to set up an art gallery. Today, his son Dadiba runs the gallery, going about its business in a similarly genuine and easy-going manner. The gallery remains integral to the growth of art in the city. An M.F. Hussain work of art on the outer wall brightens the otherwise colourless landscape here.

Opticians seem to dominate the range of commercial establishments around Flora Fountain. Three famous and equally popular optical showrooms catch your eye. Baliwala & Homi, Dinshaw & Sons (1924) and the oldest of them all, Pheroze Dastoor Opticians (1904), are landmarks in the area for their practical, 'no-frills' approach to business.

An interesting occupant of the area, that may just skip your attention, is the Pest Control of India. Housed in the Yusuf Building adjoining Readymoney Mansion, it was established way back in 1954. Another well-known city landmark in this area is the 104-year-old Davar's College of Commerce, Banking, Computers, Secretarial and Language Studies. The college was the vision of Professor Sohrab R. Davar, who at the age of twenty set up this college in a tiny room of his father's office at 9, Elphinstone Circle (now Horniman Circle) in 1900. In 1925, Davar's College shifted to the Great Western Hotel Building, Lion Gate and later to the Bank of India building at MG Road, Fort. The college moved to its present location at Mulla House, also on MG Road, in 1941. It continues to churn out hundreds of talented and aspiring secretaries and accountants year after year.

Central Bank Building

This Grade-II heritage building came up between the 1920s and '30s on N. Master Road, adjacent to Mahatma Gandhi Road. Built on a curve, it remains an impressive yellow stone building with a dome atop. It signifies a typical example of a corner building at a road junction.

Old Oriental Bank Building

Built in the late nineteenth century, this building is a Grade-III heritage structure. Lost among its brighter and up-market neighbours, it is still home to several establishments and restaurants that go back fifty years or more. This is another example of a typical corner building that uses cast iron and wooden frame balconies on its second and third floors. Today, these features seem stylistically irreplaceable because they represent the last of the frontages from the 1800s in this area.

The Fountain Restaurant and its sister concern Fountain Dry Fruits, established in 1922, are intact. So are the White House restaurant and the Kay Davy clothiers, remnants of the bygone Raj era.

HSBC, Bank of India and ANZ Grindlays

Three splendid commercial buildings that immediately catch one's eye as one stands at the Old Oriental Insurance Building are Hong Kong and Shanghai Banking Corporation, Bank of India and the ANZ Grindlays. Of the three, the ANZ Grindlays building is the

The Hong Kong and Shanghai Banking Corporation or HSBC building
▼

oldest, built in the late nineteenth century and has a beautiful baroque façade. The marbled façade of the HSBC (1920s) building is hard to miss while the Bank of India (1956) is easily the least architecturally appealing of the three, with its dull, brown stone exterior and typical masonry. Both the HSBC and ANZ Grindlays buildings are Grade-II heritage sites while the Bank of India has a Grade-III status. Nearby is the New India Assurance Building on MG Road, whose founder chairman was none other than Sir Dorab Tata. The entrance of this building is marked by geometrically precise carvings in stone, of human figures at work, to display industry, hard work and dedication - benchmarks laid by its founder while implementing his dream.

Interestingly, the enclosed street pattern arcade continues throughout MG Road as well, adding some semblance of uniformity to the otherwise jarring mix of architectural styles along this walk.

Lanes and buildings from State Bank of Hyderabad to Jehangir Building on MG Road

This short stretch is dotted by quaintly named bylanes like Ash Lane and Oak Lane. Presumably, there must have been a time when these lanes were blessed with rows of ash and oak trees! Along the Nanik Motwane Marg they all lead up to the Bombay Stock Exchange building that towers over the pedestrian throughout this walk, looming large in the background. These bylanes have an increasingly high concentration of stockbroker firms, shares and mutual fund establishments - indicative that we are in the nucleus of money county!

Khyber Restaurant

Khyber Restaurant, at MG Road, is a landmark for its delightful gastronomical fare that makes it a must-stop for those with a soft spot for North-West Frontier cuisine. Their faithful clientele continue to flock this old favourite. It is one of the city's best-known restaurants serving exquisite North-West Frontier cuisine. The restaurant has earned repute for its décor, intended to evoke the ambience of a haveli, or mansion of northern India. The reshmi kebabs and mutton rara (tender lamb chunks in a quantity of slightly spicy red gravy) are heavenly, to say the least. Its wine cellar is impressive while its dessert spread includes the divine kulfi and gajar halwa, a rich buttery pudding made in winter only from Delhi's famous red carrots.

Kapoor Lamp Shades

Probably one of the oldest and largest stores housing some of the most exquisite collections of lamps, lampshades, lighting and related accessories for homes, corporate offices, and other commercial concerns. Functioning since 1948, this store at the heart of the Kala Ghoda square, is unmistakable for its splendid window displays and classy décor. It is part of India's largest lighting retail brand, with fifteen showrooms spread across India, Sri Lanka, Kuwait, UK and the Far East. Today, it has kept up with the times and continues to draw customers to the airy, well laid-out store.

Kala Ghoda

Kala Ghoda earned its name from the statue of Albert Edward, Prince of

Wales, riding a black horse that was placed at the spot, which has now been converted to a parking lot. The statue was unveiled by Sir Richard Temple, Governor of Bombay on 26 June 1879 and stood there till 1965. Yet, the area still retains its original name.

The popular Kala Ghoda Fair is an annual event as a celebration of arts and crafts from all over India. This fair is held in Mumbai near the Jehangir Art Gallery and became a reality, thanks to the Kala Ghoda Association that was established in 1988. The aim was to improve the existing invaluable infrastructure of the

The actual statue of King Edward (after which Kala Ghoda is named) is now housed at the Veermata Jijabai Udyan in Byculla

▲
A section of Kala Ghoda

area, and give it a distinct identity as Mumbai's art district. The idea is to bring to life this vibrant art district within the city, where works by artistes in the fields of music, dance, theatre, film, and art are on display.

Rhythm House

This Mecca for music lovers is housed in the Forbes Building, built sometime in the eighteenth century. It was once the residence of wealthy citizen and merchant, Charles Forbes. In fact, the road running to the right of the building was named after him as well. Today, it is known as VB Gandhi Marg. Rhythm

House is home to, arguably, the city's most diverse and eclectic music collections - old timers and new kids on the block will willingly back this statement.

Knesseth Ell Yahoo Synagogue

A walk down VB Gandhi Marg and a sky-blue and white-coated impressive structure - the Knesseth Ell Yahoo Synagogue - leaves one spellbound. Its exterior is stunning, albeit in need of repair, and its impressive architecture sets it apart from any other structure in the Kala Ghoda sub-precinct. Built in 1884 by Jacob Sassoon, city father David Sassoon's grandson, in memory of his father Elias, it was used by the tiny Jewish population around the Fort area. Its marble teba (pulpit) is covered with a

Persian rug that dominates the cerulean interior, with its arches, columns, stained-glass windows as well as a 'high women's' gallery.

Its wide, wooden staircase also strikes the visitor, and the best part is, it is in usable condition. This three-storied Grade-II heritage structure is certainly worth a visit.

Chetana Cultural Centre

The Chetana Cultural Centre took shape in the late 1940s, as a hotbed for the art and cultural scene in the city. Famous artists, painters and poets would meet in the building where the present centre is housed. The Progressive Art Group of the 1950s always met here until the group disbanded. Over the years, its importance may have waned but it remains a prominent art and cultural centre. Today, it has a modified, more contemporary look with an art and cultural centre, a section with beautiful traditional fabrics and an extremely popular vegetarian restaurant.

Oricon Building

This Victorian-styled building to the right of the Chetana Cultural Centre is another splendid addition to the impressive architecture of the area around the Kala Ghoda square. Situated opposite Max Mueller Bhavan, the renovated building is another commercial building with its ground floor taken over by a line of swanky restaurants, boutiques and the like - similar to many other such structures in the vicinity.

Built in 1884 by Jacob Sassoon, city father David Sassoon's grandson, in memory of his father Elias, it was used by the tiny Jewish population around the Fort area

Knesseth Ell Yahoo Synagogue
▼

CULINARY MUSINGS

Just beside the Chetana Cultural Centre is the **Wayside Inn,** now converted into a Far-Eastern cuisine restaurant called Silk Route. Once upon a time, this famous streetside café and restaurant was a favourite stop for lawyers from the nearby High Court, who spent hours together debating their cases over cups of coffee. The great statesman and leader Dr. Bhim Rao Ambedkar is believed to have worked on the drafts for the Indian Constitution right here, at the historic café, still identifiable by its arch-like windows.

Max Mueller Bhavan

The city's branch of Max Mueller Bhavan was one of the six that were set up in India as part of the Goethe-Institut Inter Nationes. These centres of Indo-German study were named after the renowned German indologist Max Mueller.

Part of the Kala Ghoda Art District sub-precinct, it blends into the surroundings without much fanfare. The information centre is a treasure house of knowledge for those interested in German culture, as well as those interested in teaching and studying German as a foreign language. The centre houses over 7,000 books, videos, audio-cassettes and computer software apart from several internet-related facilities for interested visitors and students. It also organises several German film and theatre-related activities throughout the year.

◄ The Elphinstone College Building also houses the State Record Office

Jehangir Art Gallery

The heart of the Kala Ghoda square is undoubtedly the Jehangir Art Gallery. This haven for artists and sculptors is the nucleus of the city's art fraternity and was built largely due to the efforts of its founding father, the great art collector and benefactor, the second baronet Sir Cowasji Jehangir. It was due to his pioneering ability and vision that the city got its first full-fledged gallery in 1952, designed by Vanoo Bhatia and Durga Bajpai. The best collections, both from India and abroad, are displayed here. Waiting periods for prospective artists to show their collections here often run into five or even ten years! It also houses a quaint rooftop gallery as well as a café, called Samovar. This warm, laid-back eatery has grown to become the favourite stopover for celebrities from the art and entertainment world as well as collegians and office-goers, for its lip-smacking menu (topping the list are its mint tea and pakoras!) and enchanting ambience, overlooking the museum. The Jehangir Art Gallery underwent a much-needed renovation in 1990 thanks to excellent support received from concerned citizens as well as the art fraternity. Today, it holds a place of respect and importance in the city as one of its leading promoters of art.

Elphinstone College

Located opposite the Jehangir Art Gallery is the newly renovated Elphinstone Building that houses its college as well as the State Record Office. It was the first institution in India to offer university education. A life-like carved bust of Sir Cowasji Jehangir greets you at the entrance of this splendid architectural construction. The main hall is also named after him, in recognition of his contribution towards the original construction. Founded as a memorial to Governor Montstuart Elphinstone, it was divided into a school and college in 1856. The State Record Office occupies two wings in this building and preserves the oldest documents related to the East India Company's tenure in India.

The present building was completed in 1890 and is a typical Romanesque styled building, probably one of the best-preserved and renovated heritage structures within this sub-precinct. One of the oldest educational institutions in the city, the college was started as a school in 1824, founded by the Bombay Education Native Society. This Grade-I heritage site was meant to be a printing press but was converted into an education institution. By 1835, classes for degree education began and it was affiliated to the Bombay University in 1860. Its alumni reads like a page straight out of Indian history - Dadabhai Naoroji, JN Tata, Lokmanya Tilak, Badruddin Tyabji and more recently, former Chief Justice of India, Justice Y.Y. Chandrachud.

For years, this building was a sorry picture of accumulated grime and neglect. Today, thanks to a serious conservation effort, it stands as one of the most striking landmarks to benefit from the city's heritage restoration programme.

David Sassoon Library and Reading Room

This Grade-I heritage structure was built in the Venetian Gothic style in 1870. The David Sassoon Library is regarded as the oldest in the city, with visitors, researchers, students, scholars and tourists thronging the building. The library was established with generous funding by the Jewish philanthropist David Sassoon. The building stands out for its impressive yellow stone outer arcade, which gives Rampart Row its architectural distinction.

DID YOU KNOW?

In the beginning, the **David Sassoon Library & Reading Room** housed a museum and library of mechanical models and architectural designs. The structure was completed in 1879 and a complete conservation programme was undertaken over a century later, in 1996.

This Romanesque structure was built from the same yellow Malad stone that can be found in the rest of the buildings in the row - Elphinstone College, the Army and Navy Building and Watson's Hotel on Esplanade's Mansion.

Like many other buildings in the Fort area, this building too was designed by Scott McClelland and Company and built by architects J. Campbell and D.E. Gosling at the cost of Rs. 1,25,000. The ever-generous David Sassoon donated a hefty sum of Rs. 60,000 for this building, and the rest of the cost was borne by the Bombay government. The idea of the library was sounded by twelve mechanics and foremen of the Royal Mint & Government Dockyard. A statue of David is also housed within the building. The grand library was presented to the city by Sir Albert Sassoon, the son of David. In fact, it was initially called the Sassoon Mechanics Institute and then later renamed as the David Sassoon Library and Reading Room. The ground floor of this building is home to the Lund & Blockley Opticians that goes back to the early 1900s.

Army & Navy Building

Part of the troika of well-maintained heritage buildings at Kala Ghoda, the Army and Navy Building was completed in 1897. Along with David Ebenezer Gostling, a partner in his firm, F.W. Stevens designed the Army & Navy Building. It stands at the site where the former Municipal Authority's offices were located. The building was designed in an attempt to rebuild the façade. The four-storied building stood out for its splendid Italian styled exteriors and styling as well as its synthesis with neoclassical architecture. The local Malad and Porbander stone was used throughout the construction of this magnificent building. The Army & Navy Stores were a regular stop for the well-heeled British resident who frequented the departmental stores for classic furniture, furnishings and fabrics.

Today, the ground floor frontage is an upmarket department store. Thankfully, its original structure remains intact and in pristine condition, with its recently renovated freshly coated exteriors. Its porch still looks splendid with polished stone pillars. It is a Grade-II heritage structure and has successfully managed to retain its magnificent presence at Kala Ghoda.

Esplanade Mansion
(Mahendra Mansion)

Some would like to believe that it was the inspiration behind one of Jamshedji Tata's biggest projects. This mansion, built in 1868, was formerly called the Esplanade Mansion, named after the undivided Esplanade nearby. The colonial style mansion was the first ever non-frame structure to be built in the city at the time. It housed the one-time five-star hotel - Watson's - that was the pride of the city. However, the elitist hotel shut its doors to non-Europeans. Tata had to face this prejudice and vowed to build a bigger, far more luxurious hotel beside which the Watson's would pale in comparison. And build he did—the Taj Mahal Hotel! Sadly, despite its history, today this Grade-II heritage structure is one of the most neglected, run-down buildings in this part of the city.

৪০৫

The Army and Navy Building is a perfect example of a restored building in the Kala Ghoda area
▼

Rewind Time: A Walk Down Mumbai's Earliest Planned Street

(Crawford Market - Victoria [Chhatrapati Shivaji] Terminus - Anand Bhavan)

*N*ever mind the mayhem and crowds that greet you amidst over-enthusiastic sellers shouting hoarse at Crawford Market. Or the sea of humanity at Chhatrapati Shivaji Terminus that makes the Kumbh Mela crowds seem unimpressive. Forget the superfast pace you need to keep while walking down Dr. Dadabhai Naoroji Road at rush hour - at this rate qualifying for the 100 metres sprint shouldn't be too hard, you think! This is Mumbai at its crowded, most chaotic best. Yet you can slip into the past, gazing at an unbelievable diversity of architectural styles, heritage buildings and historic sights that leave you more surprised and spellbound than before. Gothic, neoclassical, Islamic, Victorian - you are bound to spot a building steeped in history at every second step throughout this walk. What amazes one is the extent to which this entire stretch fiercely guards its own history and identity. This, despite the manner in which the area might overwhelm the visitor with its congested environs and a threatening mass of humanity ready to engulf the unprepared newcomer!

APPROXIMATE DISTANCE
2.5 kilometres

APPROACH/PARKING
There is a facility for parking outside Crawford Market for those with vehicles. Yet be warned - for chances of getting any kind of space is minimal, especially at peak hours. More so, as this area is in the nucleus of the bustling retail shopping and wholesale market areas. Hopping on to any Chhatrapati Shivaji

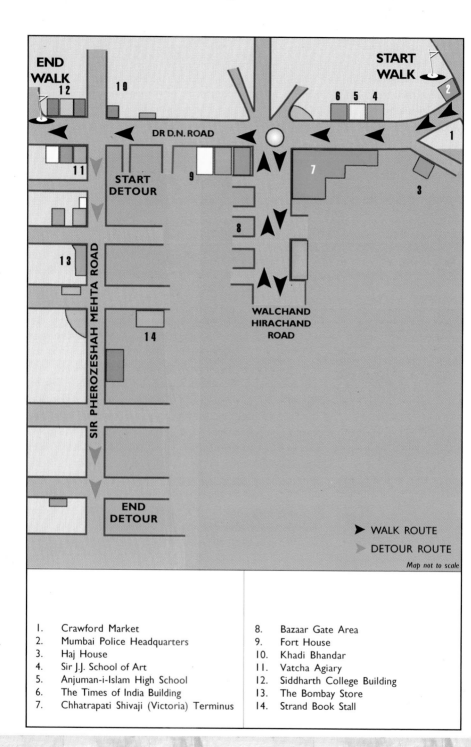

END WALK 12

10

START WALK

6 5 4

2

1

DR D.N. ROAD

11

9

START DETOUR

7

3

8

13

SIR PHEROZESHAH MEHTA ROAD

14

WALCHAND HIRACHAND ROAD

END DETOUR

▶ WALK ROUTE

▷ DETOUR ROUTE

Map not to scale

1.	Crawford Market	8.	Bazaar Gate Area
2.	Mumbai Police Headquarters	9.	Fort House
3.	Haj House	10.	Khadi Bhandar
4.	Sir J.J. School of Art	11.	Vatcha Agiary
5.	Anjuman-i-Islam High School	12.	Siddharth College Building
6.	The Times of India Building	13.	The Bombay Store
7.	Chhatrapati Shivaji (Victoria) Terminus	14.	Strand Book Stall

Terminus-bound local train would be a great idea. Alight at the terminus and proceed from its eastern exit on Dr. DN Road for a good five minutes till you sight the sprawling outer walls of the city's most famous wholesale market.

PLACES OF INTEREST

- ❖ Crawford Market
- ❖ Mumbai Police Headquarters, Lokmanya Tilak Road
- ❖ Haj House building
- ❖ Anjuman-i-Islam High School
- ❖ Sir J.J. School of Art and Architecture
- ❖ The Times of India Building
- ❖ Victoria Terminus (now renamed after Chhatrapati Shivaji)
- ❖ Bazaar Gate area (Bora Bazaar Street/ Perin Nariman Street/Mody Street)
- ❖ Rows of buildings along Dr. DN Road
- ❖ Handloom House (renovated after it was devastated by a huge fire)
- ❖ Khadi and Village Industries Commission
- ❖ Vatcha Agiary
- ❖ J.N. Petit Institute & Reading Room
- ❖ Anand Bhavan, housing Siddharth College
- ❖ **DETOUR**: Sir PM Road & its bylanes

THE WALK

This walk traverses some of the earliest roads built to decongest the exploding population that was spilling out of the Fort area. With its unique blend of old establishments and newer concerns, Mumbai conjures up images of a city holding its past and present in perfect balance. The chaos and din of the city's biggest wholesale market is the perfect starting point for this walk.

Crawford Market

The Crawford Market (renamed after Mahatma Phule) occupied an important position as it stood at the transition point between the Fort precinct and the inner city beyond. It was set up with the unflagging support and drive of the city's first Municipal Commissioner Arthur Crawford, who assumed office in 1865.

This market, now renamed after Mahatma Jyotiba Phule, the eminent social reformer, stands at the head of Dr. DN Road with Lokmanya Tilak Road running adjacent to it. The structure is a mix of Flemish and Moorish styles. This huge wholesale market is the ideal way to soak in the bustle, chaos and old-world charm of the Indian bazaar of yore. It covers an unbelievable 60,200 square metres and has a large central hall and two wings - with rows of fish, meats, vegetables, fruits, provision stalls and cutlery. Its present state however, is a common story of neglect and lack of basic civic sense, seen in many of our prized public buildings.

The main building was constructed using coarse Kurla rubble and Porbander stone as well as red stone from Bassein. The centra' hall has a drinking fountain installed with a donation from city benefactor Sir Cowasji Jehangir. It is surmounted by a thirty-nine metre (one hundred and twenty-eight feet) clock tower. The ground is paved with flagstones. Above the three gateways are panels with scenes of a group of beautiful women, representing the three principal rivers of India, sculpted by the renowned architect John Lockwood Kipling. Another gateway depicts agricultural life with peasants at work among wheat sheaves. At the western entrance, a bust of Mahatma Phule greets visitors, reminding all of the re-christened name of the market.

Nearby, on LT Road itself, is the Sardar Gruha building where the great statesman and national leader Tilak stayed and breathed his last. Fittingly, this road is named after him. It is still the official address of the *Kesari*

newspaper that Tilak started. What remains of this fierce nationalist and his legacy are a few faded photographs, letters and a majestic white bust. It was from this run-down chawl that, in 1920, Tilak's funeral procession set out. Over 2,00,000 mourners assembled on Bombay's Chowpati beach, and not a single untoward incident occured. On that fateful day his followers and well-wishers thronged this road in the pouring rain to join the procession as they bid farewell to this revolutionary leader, thinker and guide.

Mumbai Police Headquarters on Lokmanya Tilak Road

The imposing Mumbai Police Headquarters stands tall at the junction where Lokmanya Tilak Road meets with Dr. DN Road. The Office of the Commissioner of Police, Mumbai, was formally headquartered here in 1896. It was made in the Anglo-Gothic tradition of architecture and majestically stands at the site till date. The location was chosen keeping in mind the sensitivity of the juxtaposition of Mumbai's population at that time. The first Indian officer was also inducted along with the establishment of the Commissionerate in 1864. It wasn't until Independence day that the first Indian headed the police force. Rather

fittingly, this happened on 15 August 1947, when charge was officially handed over by commissioner A.E. Caffin, the last British officer, to J.S. Bharucha. The 38,000-strong Mumbai police force already has its headquarters at Crawford Market. It houses the offices of the commissioner, three joint commissioners and the crime branch.

Proceed further down Dr. DN Road and you come across rows of ammunition stores and licensed arm dealers like the Bombay Gun House and Hossanand Hormazji, and an entire block to cater to the Bengali-speaking population in the city. Indulge in some authentic, mouthwatering machcher jhol or mishti doi here at drop-dead prices. There's even a boarding and lodging facility in the aptly named Howrah House for the first-timer,

> Look closely and one comes across inscriptions from the Holy Koran on the outer façade of this marbled building

harrowed and shaken-up after alighting from the Gitanjali Express from Kolkata, at the imposing Chhatrapati Shivaji Terminus.

Haj House

On the adjacent Palton Road, where the JJ (renamed Hazrat Makhdoom Shah Mahaimi Rehmatulah Alaih) Flyover begins its climb, is the towering presence of the Haj House. This cream-coloured building is a pivotal centre for the city's Muslim population. Look closely and one comes across inscriptions from the Holy Koran on the outer façade of this marbled building. However, the structure has had a negative impact on the architectural style of the stretch from Crawford Market to Victoria Terminus due to its high-rise nature, commercial design and distinct modern façade; it stands out for its rather modern construction, that differs from the rest of the old-styled buildings in the vicinity.

The towering twenty-one-storey building was funded and erected by the Central Haj Committee and is one of the most impressive modern buildings built by the community in the country. Haj pilgrims from within and outside the state are accommodated in this Haj House. The government also makes arrangements for customs and immigration clearance and the issue of foreign exchange. This apart, pilgrims even get their boarding passes at the building before setting off for their holy pilgrimage to Mecca.

Walk down Palton Road and it meets with Dr. DN Road near the JJ Flyover. Here, one sees Geoffrey House. Interestingly, this Victorian building, with grey stone exteriors was and still remains a family clinic meant for industrial labourers in the city. Further ahead, parallel to the Chhatrapati Shivaji Terminus, are the staid-looking Central Railway offices that sprung up towards the middle of the twentieth century to cater to the burgeoning pressure on the Central Railway.

Anjuman-i-Islam High School

On the opposite side, beside the Sir JJ School of Art and Architecture, stands the impressive Anjiman-i-Islam High School designed in the Indo-Saracenic style by a renowned architect of the time, John Adams. Built in 1893, it proved a turning point for the growth of Muslim culture, education and

◀ *A visually inspiring view of the Haj House*

Carvings along the outer façade of the Haj House
▼

services in the city. Its large central hall originally had a purdah gallery for the first Muslim women who received an education. The school has an impressive thirty-eight-metre high tower capped with a dome and three turrets supporting smaller domes of Porbander stone. The structure also has traces of Indo-Islamic design on its exteriors.

Today, the school is a central point for Islamic education in the city. It is also home to the Allana English High School and the Akbar Peerbhoy Polytechnic, both housed within its campus. There is an unmistakable uniformity in the construction of both buildings.

Sir JJ School of Art and Architecture

The country's premier art institute, this school bears the name of the renowned city father and benefactor Sir Jamsetjee Jeejeebhoy. Its first pupils were admitted way back in 1857. But the present building, with sloping tiled roofs and rounded pillars, was built much later, in 1877. Many public and private buildings throughout west India owe their murals, exterior façades, paintings, carvings and decorative

stonework to students of this institution. Sir John Lockwood Kipling, writer Rudyard Kipling's father, was its principal in the school's early days.

The Times of India Building

The plaque outside the main entrance informs you that the foundation stone of this magnificent landmark was laid on the 'First day of the 20th Century'. Inside this building, the English language daily newspaper *The Times of India*, along with several of its sister publications—weeklies, magazines and other journals—takes shape with assembly-line uniformity and clockwork precision. On

◀ *Islamic architecture is an obvious feature of the Anjuman-i-Islam High School building*

The Sir JJ School of Art ▶ and Architecture continues to churn out artistic and creative talent today, as it has since its inception in 1857

The Times of India building is fondly referred to as the 'Old Lady of Boribunder'

◄ *The famous red telephone booth outside the TOI building is a product of the city's recent tryst with modern architectural enterprise*

The hallowed inner sanctum of the ►
Chhatrapati Shivaji Terminus

November 3, 1838, a bi-weekly called *The Bombay Times and Journal of Commerce* was first published in the city for English-language readers. In 1850, it became a daily with J.E. Brennan as its first editor. Two years later, it was absorbed into *The Bombay Standard and Bombay Telegraph and Courier*. Finally in 1861, its name was changed to *The Times of India* under editor Robin Knight.

It was from the terrace of this building that in 1921 a special programme of music was broadcast on the radio with the help of the Post and Telegraph Department for the Governor of Mumbai, Sir George Lloyd, who tuned into the broadcast from Pune. Today, the English version of the newspaper reaches a readership of (approximately) 2.4 million, while its versions in two regional languages reach nearly a million readers across the country.

Victoria Terminus (renamed after Chhatrapati Shivaji)

Paeans have been written in the past and to this day on the splendour of the city's most recognisable landmark, on par with the Gateway of India. Sir F.W. Stevens' brilliant work remains unrivalled in terms of architectural genius, detail and magnitude.

From the later part of 1878, the ten-year span of construction began. F.W. Stevens was officially 'lent' by the Government to the Railway Company for this particular construction. The entire structural cost amounted to an estimated sixteen to thirty-six lakh rupees! It was planned at a pivotal spot between the docks and the harbour. The spot was selected so that travellers moving from the Suez eastward to India could board a train from the Terminus towards any place on the mainland.

Students and professors from the Sir JJ School of Art designed and decorated its interiors, under the direct supervision of F.W. Stevens and John Griffiths, his superintendent. Richly coloured Italian marble, Porbander and Seoni sandstone, Indian blue stone and teakwood were used for its grand interiors. Thomas Earp used

▲
Buildings representative of the architecture seen on Dr. DN Road

Bath stone for many of its exceptional sculptural projects. A statue of Queen Victoria was erected at the second level. Other statues include those in honour of the early railway directors as well as those depicting sixteen castes of India. Besides this, there are peacock tympanums on the frontal façades under the arches that add a striking 'Indianness' to the structure. Extreme richness of detail was the hallmark. Statues projecting Commerce, Agriculture and Civil Engineering can be seen at the entrance. The entire structure is surmounted by a large figure depicting Progress atop the dome. Other figures representing Science and Trade are at the ground level. It was eventually completed in May 1888. Not surprisingly, it was regarded as the second-most photographed building in Asia in the nineteenth century, after the Taj Mahal.

Bazaar Gate (parallel to Dr. DN Road - Perin Nariman Road/Bora Bazaar Street/Mody Street)

As one departs from Victoria Terminus via the eastern exit near the General Post Office, it is easy to find the crowded Bazaar Gate area. The earliest developments in the Fort area took place in the Bazaar Gate area where most of the commercial buildings were built up to two or three levels. The spread of the bazaar-type street pattern was synonymous with urban development throughout Indian towns at the time and this pattern found its way throughout the Bazaar Gate area. Unfortunately, the unique street pattern as well as Gothic buildings built alongside are lost among the roadside stalls and hawkers that have occupied its arcade space.

These streets still recapture the flavour of the original 'Black' or 'Native' Town. It was here immediately outside the Fort walls that the middle and lower-class Indian population resided. Today's Bora Bazaar Street, Mody Street, Perin Nariman Street and portions of Mint Street cover this area. These narrow, crowded and bustling lanes transport the pedestrian to a different time. Never mind the huge, ugly concrete structures that have sprung all over these older parts of the Fort precinct. By the mid-eighteenth century this area witnessed a trade boom as communities from Gujarat and central India descended into the city to seek their fortunes. Bora Bazaar Street gets its name from the Bohra (or Bohri) sect, who are Gujarati-speaking Muslims. The largest section is concentrated in Mumbai, towards the northern end of the

DID YOU KNOW?

The fire brigade was built within the **Bora Bazaar** area, where several fires had taken place largely due to the badly ventilated constructions and poor approach roads built in a high density street pattern. Overall, the site had inadequate facilities for fire safety, and the need to have a fire brigade within the area was considered of immense importance.

Fort, and hence bears the name of the community.

Closer to the railway terminus, Blackie House (built in the 1920s) on Walchand Hirachand Marg comes across as a rather ominous looking black stone building. These commercial premises, along with the Bazaar Gate Police Station (built in the late 1800s) housed in the neighbouring grey stone building, are two of the larger constructions at the entrance of the congested Fort market area beyond it. The Indian Globe Chambers and the City Lodge buildings, also standing opposite the western exit of the terminus are some of the structures built in the colonial style of architecture, unseen in the Bazaar Gate area.

The Bazaar Gate area stood as the headquarters of the wealthy Shroff community who were considered the backbone of the Indian banking businesses in the nineteenth and early twentieth centuries. Naturally, the capital market remained under their control. Many of the private moneylenders also resided here. Their hundis (a draft) were honoured and accepted throughout India. It is believed that many of them even helped the Bombay

Government when they were in dire financial crisis!

Row of buildings along Dr. Dadabhai Naoroji Road (formerly Hornby Road)

Dr. DN Road runs on a north-south axis between the Victoria Terminus and Flora Fountain. Despite the architectural diversity of the area, it shows signs of homogeneity because of the uniform street-line pattern. Here, the arcade was made mandatory for all buildings and served as a uniform element at the street level. This road provides a fine stretch of heritage buildings for the discerning eye and the newcomer alike. It is still considered one of the most successfully designed and controlled streets in the city. The area displays a variety of architectural styles in its public, commercial and corporate buildings ranging from the grand Gothic, Victorian and Renaissance designs to a mix of styles that came to be termed as colonial.

A note of caution here - walking down Dr. DN Road while on this heritage walk requires you to pay close attention to buildings on both sides of the road! Chances of missing the odd building are high, especially since they stand alarmingly close to each other. The first in the line is the crumbling (currently undergoing renovation) Empire Building that formerly housed the New Empire Café and Stores, one of the many Parsi restaurants that had to make way for modern fast food establishments throughout the city. Built in the early twentieth century, the much-needed initial conservation work on this run-down structure was completed in 1998. Walk down this road and on either side the common feature is, undoubtedly, the uniform street arcade pattern. The Killick House building that houses the State Bank of India

service branch (also under renovation), Wheeler Building and the Kodak Building are some of the obvious examples.

On the opposite side of the road are rows of old-styled watch and eye wear establishments, like the Eastern Watch Co. and F.C. Whitten & Co. In the same line are a few older constructions - the Indian Globe Chambers building, Commissariat Building, Bachchubai Building, Sonico Shopping Centre and Ravi Building - a virtual haven for photographers, with an unbelievable range of cameras and related equipment. Nearby, in the same row, is the Saroosh Building where you chance upon a dusty board, which informs the passerby that the original 'Light of Asia' restaurant, was set up here, way back in 1912!

Along this stretch, another building that stands out for its architecture and grandeur is the Sir JJ Parsi Benevolent Institute, which was an educational institution founded in 1875. Its sharp, distinctive stonework is reminiscent of the Renaissance style. This Grade II heritage building is noted for its broad, laid-out street arcade at the front as well as historic Zoroastrian inscriptions on its exteriors.

On both sides of the road are rows of shops selling anything from rare Bhutanese postal stamps, sleazy magazines, snazzy-looking handycams and rare hardbound manuals on architecture and design. The legendary Taraporevala Book Store is one of the oldest occupants in the New Assurance Building. Next is the neoclassical Canada Building that originally housed the Sun Life Assurance of Canada, and thus adopted the name. The freshly done brick-red and white coloured exterior of the Navsari Building stands out among its neighbours. It houses arguably the oldest functioning lift in India, which is supposed to be over a hundred years old! Next is the General Assurance Building and the Cox Building that takes its

▲
One of the many impressive buildings on Dr. DN Road

name from the age-old Cox & Kings Travels, its oldest occupant. A majority of buildings along this road were designed by British firm Gostling and Morris, and their stamp of design can be spotted throughout this road. They were largely neoclassical, functional constructions with the typical enclosed street-arcade pattern.

The famous Lawrence & Mayo opticians, established in 1877, is housed in the Macmillan Buildings. The plaque on its façade informs you that British Prime Minister Harold Macmillan's publishing house was once housed here, hence the name stayed on. Lawrence & Mayo shifted to its current address in 1901.

An amusing anecdote is also related on the plaque below. Apparently, a pair of spectacles mysteriously went missing from the showroom window at Lawrence & Mayo. After much delay and worry, they were recovered from a crow's nest in the neighbouring Grindlays Building!

On the other side is the recently renovated Eruchshaw Building, opposite Khadi Bhandar. Built in 1817, it is one of the earliest establishments of the area, much before Hornby Road (now called Dr. DN Road) was fully structured. These commercial premises stand out for the imposing cast iron structure with detailed glazed tiling, engraved glass and a period lift-cage. The building houses a sacred well in its inner courtyard, far from the gaze of the maddening crowds and traffic that surrounds it from the outside. The Peninsula House and Cama House exhibit a similar grandeur, albeit in ruin and need of restoration. The Residency Hotel at the junction of Dr. DN Road and Rustom Sidhwa Road was another restaurant for the well-heeled British resident of the city. Today, it still has an old-world charm the moment you step in.

The Piramal Building beside Eruchshaw also forms part of the uniform arcade street pattern of this road. Situated on the eastern side of DN Road is another famous address. It is the nineteenth century construction known as the Fort House that was the town residence of the famous citizen, first baronet Sir Jamsetji Jeejeebhoy. It was built way back in 1834 and was once considered the most impressive residence in the Fort. In fact, his residence was illuminated for the proclamation of Queen Victoria as the Empress of India on 1 November 1858! This three-storied mansion had a classical façade and broad terraces. Many decades later, it was eventually converted to Evans, Fraser & Co. which was an upmarket and extremely popular department store during the British Raj. Post-independence, it was converted into the Handloom House, until most of this building was razed in a devastating fire. Today, the building has been rebuilt and represents a near-perfect replication of its previous architectural splendour.

Khadi Bhandar and Village Commission

The landmark along this stretch is undoubtedly the Khadi Bhandar, housed in the Jeevan Udyog Building. Formerly known as the Whiteway and Laidlaw Stores in the post-independence era, it was a popular stop for British residents in the city. Also designed by Gostling & Morris in a mix of Indian and Neo-Classical architecture, its premises once housed the photography studio of the great Raja Deen Dayal. In fact,

it was originally known as the Metropolitan Insurance Buildings.

Vatcha Agiary

The Vatcha Agiary stands near the point where DN Road turns into Sir PM Road as one nears Flora Fountain, and is located inside the Kermani Building. This Grade-III heritage structure was completed on 19 May 1910 in the heart of the city's commercial district and is an important place of worship for the Zoroastrian community. Even pedestrians and office-goers caught in rush hour do not fail to notice the huge Assyrian stone façades that dominate the entrance of this otherwise rather simple building. The agiary lies safely tucked inside the confines of a quieter world within its sombre exteriors.

JN Petit Institute and Reading Room

At the junction where Maharshi Dadhichi Road meets Dr. DN Road is the imposing JN Petit Institute and Reading Room, which is one

The JB Petit Institute and Reading Room on Dr. DN Road
▼

The Thomas Cook ▶
Building on
Dr. DN Road

of the best examples of restoration along the stretch. The impeccable condition of the building is worth seeing, thanks to HSBC's pioneering work. Its brick-red panels stand out and the outer façade and surroundings still retain their original grandeur. This Grade-II heritage structure was built in 1898 and was extended to its present size in 1938. The building is noticeable for its striking polychromatic exteriors and well-maintained ground floor arcade, in comparison with many neglected buildings in the vicinity.

Next is Cook's Building, home to another famous city travel house - Thomas Cook. Standard Buildings are home to a famous landmark as we near Flora Fountain - the sprawling Great Western Stores (Proprietors F.D. Mehta & Co.) that remains one of the city's oldest footwear retailers, in operation since 1916. Today the 'Bata Shoes' hoarding outside this store, housed in the twin Standard Buildings, cannot but catch your eye as it did all those years ago.

Anand Bhavan - Siddharth College

This early twentieth century commercial and educational premise, a Grade-II heritage site, stands out for its freshly-coated exteriors - in complete contrast to the many dilapidated, neglected buildings on DN Road. It has managed to retain its group value with the rest of the arcade-street front pattern, despite undertaking recent repairs and renovations. The Siddharth College is housed within Anand Bhavan, in what was formerly called Albert Building. The college is closely

▲
*Anand Bhavan, home to Siddharth College, on
Dr. DN Road*

associated with the great Dr. BR Ambedkar,
who worked ceaselessly to establish this
institution. The neoclassical building sports a
fresh coat of yellow paint, with buff basalt
façades and semi-circular arches.

DETOUR: Sir Pherozeshah Mehta Road and its bylanes

Sir PM Road was developed as a link to
connect the newly laid Ballard Estate with the
busy, commercial DN Road. This road was
built in the 1920s. Most buildings along this
road were designed in the Art Deco style
prevalent throughout the city at that time.
Most of them were of uniform height - five or
six storied buildings. Their typical pattern
divided the southern Fort area from the dense

Bazaar Gate area. In fact, this road was created
by razing down some of the more congested
parts of the Bazaar Gate.

The first buildings that came up in the
1930s were constructed for the Bombay
Mutual Fund, where the ground floor was
leased to the National City Bank of New York.
If you are an old-time Mumbaiite, as you walk
down, several favourite landmarks come
rushing to your mind. Like the Twin Records
Depot, in the Kermani Building, established
way back in the 1940s. Today, this music store
is a poor shadow of its former glory when
music lovers from all over the city and beyond
would gather at the store that housed the
latest LPs, gramophone records, gramophones
and old-fashioned audio tapes! Another music
store that managed to survive is Hiro Music,
housed in the United Bank of India Building.

As one walks down this road, it becomes
clear that this road could have well been

renamed 'Bank Street' for the large number of banking establishments jostling for space here. Like the UTI Bank inside, the Bell Building got its name from the still-standing Bell Plaza (another department store from the mid-twentieth century). Other financial and banking firms include the Bank of Tokyo, Citibank and the LIC Building. Not to forget some of the oldest seafood restaurants in the city - Mahesh Lunch Home (on Cawasjee Patel Road) and Apoorva (on Brelvi Road). Both remain popular stopovers among the city's seafood-loving population. The Mocambo Café (on Cawasjee Patel Road) is a favourite among beer guzzlers and office crowds for its reasonable prices. Another interesting landmark is The Bombay Store (formerly Bombay Swadeshi Stores) founded by Lokmanya Tilak to encourage people to use Indian-made goods. Housed in the Western India Building, today the store has metamorphosed itself into a tourist's delight - Indian jewellery, artifacts, clothing, footwear and so on make for a great shopping experience.

A walk down Sir PM Road would be incomplete without a stopover at the Strand Book Stall. Started by T. Shanbagh on 20 November 1948, this was a tiny book stall catering to a miniscule yet highly enthusiastic bunch of book lovers that borrowed its name from the nearby (now defunct) Strand Cinema. Four years later, the store moved to its current address on Brelvi Road. Notwithstanding the space constraints, readers throng this bookstore with ever-increasing interest. A few exquisite handicraft stores catering to the discerning tourist also dot this road. One shouldn't forget the tiny rubber stamp makers, book and computer stationery stores that lie tucked away on each of these bylanes off Sir PM Road. Hordes of food

DID YOU KNOW?

Alice Buildings beside the Vatcha Agiary on Dr. DN Road was gutted by a ravaging fire sometime ago. This building originally had a sturdy stone faced exterior and the typical uniform street arcade pattern architecture. Sadly, its renovation has been extremely slow and what stands now are temporary stalls that have mushroomed all along its frontage. It once housed a popular Irani café that was also lost to the same fire that ravaged the entire building in 1973. Interestingly, in the old days when the Fort walls were intact, a smaller gate for pedestrians stood opposite Alice Buildings for entry and exit to the Fort!

stalls have sprung up along this road to cater largely to the office crowds at lunch hours. Everything from fiery-hot 'Shezwan Chaineeze' food to the 'gorge-at-your-own-risk' pav bhaji or the deceptively-inviting sugarcane juices are available among a melee of gastronomical delights for the 'care-a-damn' foodie! Come lunch time and the area is abuzz with an astonishing number of bustling mobile kitchens catering to the hungry thousands. Without doubt, the motto here reads loud and clear - 'Live to eat, repent later!'

ೞಐ

A Hidden Past: Walking Along Old Dockyard Road, The Gateway & Beyond

(Old Customs House - Gateway of India - Radio Club)

 ike a dazzling maiden proudly watching over her muse, the island city's love affair with the Arabian Sea is the stuff legends are made of. This walk is parallel to the sea that remains unseen to the eye until you approach the Gateway. Yet you experience a steady sea breeze throughout, making it a worthy companion and guide all the way. The walk takes you through some of the oldest parts of the early city - roads and structures that have stoically stood through the city's fascinating history for over four centuries. Mumbai's most famous landmark, the Gateway of India, is the high point of this walk. And just as you recover from its gigantic, awe-inspiring presence with the twin Taj Mahal hotels in the background, you are left marvelling at one of the most spectacular promenades in India, the Apollo Bunder. And there is much more for the curious mind. Old, nondescript buildings with intriguing pasts, its busy natural harbour and the Naval Dockyard, sleepy lanes of Colaba that take the reader on a delightful journey of emporiums, curio shops and run-down colonial homes with rickety staircases. Above all, an eclectic mix of the old and new worlds.

APPROXIMATE DISTANCE
3 kilometres

APPROACH/PARKING
The best way to reach the first point of this walk would be to board any of the BEST buses (numbers 2, 3, 108) from the General Post Office bus stop outside Chhatrapati Shivaji Terminus and alight at the Reserve Bank of India stop.

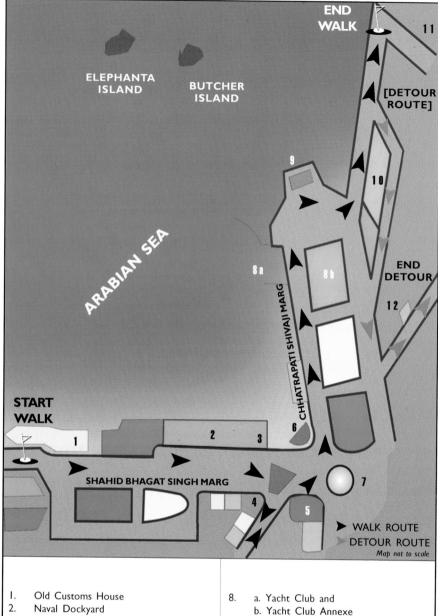

ELEPHANTA ISLAND

BUTCHER ISLAND

ARABIAN SEA

END WALK

[DETOUR ROUTE]

11

10

9

8 a

8 b

END DETOUR

12

CHHATRAPATI SHIVAJI MARG

START WALK

1

2   3

6

SHAHID BHAGAT SINGH MARG

4

5

7

WALK ROUTE
DETOUR ROUTE

Map not to scale

1.	Old Customs House	
2.	Naval Dockyard	
3.	Lion Gate	
4.	Church of St. Andrew's	
5.	Bombay Natural History Society	
6.	Maharashtra State Police Headquarters	
7.	Wellington Fountain	
8.	a. Yacht Club and	
	b. Yacht Club Annexe	
9.	Gateway of India	
10.	Taj Mahal Hotel &	
	Taj Intercontinental	
11.	Radio Club	
12.	Bade Miya	

Alternatively, taxe a taxi from the Chhatrapati Shivaji Terminus to Horniman Circle and commence your walk at the Old Customs House, barely a minute away. Parking around the Horniman Circle Gardens would be a good bet if you have your own vehicle and start early, before the office traffic moves in.

PLACES OF INTEREST

- ❖ Old Customs House
- ❖ Writer's Building
- ❖ Admiralty Building
- ❖ Cama Oriental Institute
- ❖ Scotts Kirk Church
- ❖ Lion Gate - Naval Dockyard
- ❖ Bombay Natural History Society
- ❖ Southern end of Fort near Rampart Row
- ❖ Maharashtra Police Headquarters
- ❖ Row of buildings along Apollo Pier (now CST Marg)
- ❖ Yacht Club & its premises
- ❖ Gateway of India
- ❖ Taj Mahal Hotel and Taj Intercontinental
- ❖ The Victoria
- ❖ The lighthouses of Mumbai harbour
- ❖ Apollo Bunder promenade
- ❖ The Radio Club
- ❖ **DETOUR**: Henry Street - Mereweather Road - Tullock Road

THE WALK

With the sea as an unseen presence in the background, your walk begins in arguably one of the oldest parts of the city - the Old Customs House on Shahid Bhagat Singh Marg, beside the Asiatic Society of Mumbai. This area to the south of the Town Hall is known for a uniform street pattern replete with a continuous line of similarly structured buildings - most of which have disappeared. The initial part of this walk covers an area formerly known as the Dockyard Road. One of the gates of the Fort walls - the Apollo

Gate - stood here as an entry point for the Colaba and Old Woman's Islands when Mumbai was a divided land mass of many islands.

Old Customs House

The Old Customs House was built between 1710-14 by the Portuguese as barracks for their soldiers. Today, it is recognised as a Grade-I heritage structure. One of the oldest, still-standing structures within the city, this stone structure was built by the East India Company after the islands passed over to the British from the Portuguese. It resembles the earliest stone-faced period building in the area. The crest of the Company can be seen in bas-relief on the exterior façade within the terrace of the stone porch. At one time, this building was abuzz with a different kind of activity, filled with muccadams who cleared goods, coolies (porters) who hauled goods up and down its staircases and godowns, chittiwalas who made import and export manifests and the middlemen along with the small class traders.

Today, this building houses several important administrative sections including the Office of the Collector and District Magistrate, Mumbai city, the Deputy Inspector General of Registration and the Office of the Special Inspector General of Police/Traffic.

Walk further down Shahid Bhagat Singh Marg and an entire stretch of uniform buildings meets the eye. Some, like the Khattau Building, Ali Building and Sharif House, show minute traces of Indo-Islamic architecture.

Writer's Building (also called Old Writer's Home)

The Writer's Building stands at the point where the Bombay Samachar Marg meets the Shahid Bhagat Singh Marg. This is a run-

The Writer's Building is a typical example of the earliest stock of British residential and administrative architecture. This large structure is extremely plain and appears quite unassuming, due to its purely functional nature. However, it is of immense historic importance as it housed the old Secretariat of the East India Company and later, British Government clerks and writers (hence the name of the building) during the period of their rule in the city.

Admiralty House

One of the most defining landmarks that bear testimony to the city's passage in time is this rather nondescript Grade-I heritage structure down Shahid Bhagat Singh Marg. Today, a large board that reads Great Western Hotel precariously hangs at the entrance of this structure in dire need of repair and restoration. Built in 1715, it initially served as the Residence of the Admiral from 1764-92, hence the original name is commonly used in reference. In 1800, it became the Court of the First Recorder of Bombay and remained the Chief Court of Bombay until 1879. This

down, eighteenth century colonial, yet functional, structure that almost skips the eye. On closer scrutiny, semi-circular arches at ground level give the onlooker an idea of how most buildings from the 1800s would have appeared. It is representative of the uniform building style, unseen in other parts of the city that dotted this entire stretch till the Scotts Kirk Church. External teakwood fluted columns can still be seen on the outer façade of the building. It included carved and pierced woodwork in its wooden frames and balconies.

◄ *The Great Western Hotel now stands in the building that was once the historic Admiralty House*

building also served as the second Government House (the first was within the Bombay Castle) and remained the official residence of the Governor till 1829. In 1883, the building was leased and eventually purchased by a wealthy Parsi, Jewanjee Guzdar, who converted it into the Great Western Hotel.

This structure is almost overshadowed by the din and gloomy surroundings. The massive symmetrical building has a central verandah at the ground floor that also serves as an entrance to the foyer. The teakwood balcony, an integral part of the architecture found among most buildings on this stretch, is seen on the top floor. According to records, the main roof on the topmost floor had a series of dormer windows that offered an unobstructed view of the harbour in the past. The main building, much altered, is what we see today.

Ironically, just beside this crumbling structure is the plush fashion house Ensemble, started by a famous Indian fashion designer. It plays host to a range of regional as well as international fashion labels. This studio, which is over ten years old, was one of the city's earliest and has subtly merged into the environs of its historic neighbours.

Cama Oriental Institute

Standing beside the Church of St. Andrew's, is the freshly-renovated yellow building that houses the Cama Oriental Institute. Built in 1930, the institute is a social and educational establishment engaged in research and studies. Assyrian pillars stand at the external façade of this otherwise plain, utilitarian Grade-III heritage building. Today, it plays host to exhibitions, seminars and similar public events.

Interestingly, this institute stands on the site where the old Ice House once stood.

The Ice House was built in 1863 with a public subscription of Rs. 10,000. The higher levels of this spherical building are accessible by a circular iron staircase. Once upon a time, ice was imported from America and stored here. However, when the manufacture of ice began in Mumbai, import of ice was discontinued from America. The Ice House building was demolished and in its place the Cama Institute was built.

Scotts Kirk Church (Church of St. Andrew's)

This church overlooking Lion Gate was once regarded as the second-most important church in the area after St. Thomas Cathedral, and is situated nearby. It was the second church to come up in the Fort and was completed between 1818 and 1821, while its spire came up in 1823. Scotts Kirk was the earliest Gregorian church in the city built with towering white pillars that gave the entrance an air of resplendent grace. This spire was replaced four years later when the original was destroyed by lightning. The teakwood frame building stands out with its ornate wooden balconies, decorated façades and tiled roofs - reminiscent of a time when this church was representative of the first recognisable style of British architecture in the city.

By 1858, the church along with the Old Ice House, the Hornby House and the Clock Tower of the docks formed a familiar and important row of buildings along the Old Dockyard Road. Today services in this colonial-styled church are few and not many are aware of its historic significance in the area and city at large. Thankfully, due to the intervention of several concerned citizens and heritage associations, its upkeep is in safe hands. It was conferred the Urban Heritage Award in 1993.

Naval Dockyard - Lion Gate

The Naval Dockyard, a Grade-I heritage site, traces its earliest root as early as 1735 and it developed into a fully-functional dockyard by 1798. It was among the confines of this military construction that the city emerged from a dull trading seaport to India's busiest natural harbour and port. 1735 was a defining year in the Naval Dockyard's history. The original dockyard was constructed by Lowjee Nusserwanjee Wadia, the master ship builder who came from Gujarat and set up the first dry dock that supported a natural harbour in Asia, in 1735, at the request of the British East India Company. The then Governor Gerald Aungier, declared the Bombay harbour as 'the fairest, largest and securest in all these parts of India.' Two more dry docks were built in 1750 and 1765 by the

The main entrance to the high-security zone of the Naval Dockyard, at Lion Gate
▼

same person who built the dockyard from scratch and even selected the site.

The Naval Dockyard was officially commissioned in 1750. Apart from ship repairs, new ships were also built here throughout the 1700s and 1800s. Between 1736 and 1800,

The then Governor Gerald Aungier declared the Bombay harbour as 'the fairest, largest and securest in all these parts of India.' Two more dry docks were built in 1750 and 1765

as many as 114 vessels of different sizes and specifications were built here. Today, this high-security shipyard undertakes maintenance and refit facilities of Indian naval ships and submarines docked in the city's natural harbour.

The dock frontage along Shahid Bhagat Singh Marg, forms the stretch that remained untouched over the pa st 200 years. City historian Foy Nissen, when he speaks about the Dockyard Road, calls it the 'oldest surviving street line vista in Bombay.' This stretch has remained intact since the 1700s. The Bell Clock Tower within the Naval Dockyard enclosure is the one consistent feature that is a silent bystander from the past. Though

The Church of St. Andrew's
▼

non-functional today, its wind compass still operates on the whims of the Arabian Sea breeze.

South-western half of Fort (Rampart Row)

Walk past the Scotts Kirk Church, towards the back end of Rampart Row (extreme end of K. Dubash Marg) and one is suddenly exposed to an entirely different landscape. Dull, dilapidated buildings emerging from the staid, uniform street pattern along the Old Dockyard Road make way for an expanse of broad roads, cobbled pavements and freshly-painted façades. The change is simply fascinating - an interesting mix of colonial and vernacular architecture. This street was once home to several mercantile offices in the pre-Independence era.The 'look' of several such buildings remains unchanged, though rows of parked cars along these buildings prevent one from getting an unobstructed view of these impressive, well-maintained buildings. A striking example of the commercial premises is Ador House which is home to offices, consulates and plush new restaurants catering to the tourist and the well-heeled Mumbaiite.

Bombay Natural History Society - Hornbill House

Opposite the Lion Gate is the site on which the Bombay Natural History Society is located. This seemingly low-profile society is in fact, the largest non-government organisation (NGO) in the Indian sub-continent, which is engaged in nature conservation research. A name synonymous with the Society is its late president and legendary ornithologist Dr. Salim Ali, who always backed conservation based on scientific research.

DID YOU KNOW?

The area where today's **Rampart Row** stands was once the heart of the rope-making industry. Formerly called Rope-walk Lane, it was an industry closely connected with the docks and simultaneously grew as the dockyard's importance increased. The industry was extended and renovated in 1760. Here, cables and hemp ropes for the Royal Navy, the Honorary Company's Service and merchant vessels were exported. Ropes of coconut fibre and coir were also manufactured for the local industry and trade.

As early as 1883, eight residents of Bombay (now Mumbai) decided to form a Society to study Natural History. The team, comprising of six Englishmen and two Indians, met for the first time on 15 September 1883 at the Victoria and Albert Museum (now renamed Dr. Bhau Daji Museum inside the Byculla Zoo premises). Together, they constituted themselves as the Bombay Natural History Society. The intention was to regularly meet and exchange notes related to natural history, exhibit interesting specimens and share ideas. From 1883, the Society was located first on Forbes Street and later, Apollo Street. By then, there was a great need to have a museum to store the invaluable collections and treasures of the Society.

It was much later, on 15 August 1905 that the Government agreed to have a permanent memorial to commemorate the visit of the Royal Highnesses, the Prince and Princess of Wales to the City and Presidency in the form of a public museum and library. In 1957, an agreement between the Museum and the State

Government was concluded, as a result of which the Society severed its connections with the Museum. The State Government agreed to fund the Society's collections apart from exhibits at the Museum and the establishment to maintain them. The Indian Government stepped in and ensured that this Society stayed alive. It offered to fund the setting up of 'Hornbill House' to house the Bombay Natural History Society. *Hornbill* is also the name of the magazine published by the BNHS.

With a grant of Rs. 3.34 lakhs from the Indian Ministry of Scientific Research and Cultural Affairs, Hornbill House was built by the Prince of Wales Museum and completed in 1965. Hornbill House is named after the Society's mascot, the Great Indian Hornbill.

The Royal Alfred Sailor's Home now houses the state's police headquarters
▼

Maharashtra Police Headquarters

This structure was formerly known as the Royal Alfred Sailors' Home and also served as the Old Council Hall prior to its present status. The name commemorated the visit of His Royal Highness Prince Alfred, Duke of Edinburgh to the city in 1870. The Maharaja of Baroda along with the Duke, laid the foundation stone. This Grade-I heritage Gothic-styled building was completed in 1876 and served as an important landmark at the Colaba junction facing the Wellington Fountain. F.W. Stevens designed this magnificent structure, superseding the earlier proposal by John Macvicar Anderson for the site. The Royal Alfred Sailors' Home housed seventy-eight seamen in those early days.

This huge, grey, stone building's exterior is faced with blue and white basalt. The white corners of Porbander stone are the creation of Sir Lockwood Kipling, Rudyard Kipling's father. The building is replete with carvings by students from the Sir JJ School of Art, under supervision from Sir John. Burjorjie Nowrojie of Sir JJ School, designed the impressive iron castings, ornamental ironwork and the staircase railings within the building. J. Macfarlene & Co. of Glasgow undertook the manufacture of the iron gates at the entrance hall as well as the arched openings on the ground floor.

The Office of the Commissioner of Police, Mumbai, was formally headquartered here in 1896. It was chosen as the State Police Headquarters due to its nodal location and proximity to the harbour and the Dockyard, the Gateway, the Fort as well as the maidans. Designed by architect F. W. Stevens, it was built on the razed site of Mendham's Point, which was Mumbai's earliest British cemetery. It was taken over by the Government in 1928 and a Council Chamber for the Bombay Legislature was built at the back. Later, the Maharashtra State Legislature and Council met here. In fact, there was a time when the famous seafarer and writer Joseph Conrad stayed within its confines. His experiences here inspired the story of the sailing ship in his book *The Nigger of the Narcissus.*

Opposite the headquarters is the well-laid out Wellington Fountain that was built in 1865. Today, this important junction at the entrance of the Colaba Causeway is renamed as the Shyama Prasad Mukherji Marg. The fountain, like several other monuments was built to commemorate the visits of the Duke of Wellington to the city in 1861 and 1864.

Row of buildings along Apollo Pier Road

As you move out of the Police Headquarters, you need to take a turn into the Chhatrapati Shivaji Marg that heads towards the Gateway of India. This road was built with the idea to give a direct view of the grand structure. Yet design plans went slightly awry and when the Gateway was eventually completed, this road did not give the pedestrian a direct view of George Wittet's famous creation!

An impressive row of three-four storied buildings line this stretch. The first is the one that houses the popular Central Cottage Industries Emporium. It was recently renovated and painted, complementing its outer façade and old-world charm. So also with Dhanraj Mahal beside it, with its bold brown exteriors and subtle Art Deco style of architecture. There was a time when it was the costliest and largest single residential cum commercial complex that came up on the site of the former Watsons Annexe. Another noticeable structure on the opposite side of this road is the Kalapesi Building, near the Regal Cinema complex.

Yacht Club and its premises

En route to the Gateway, along the Chhatrapati Shivaji Marg are the premises of the Yacht Club, its club house and its other premises. Built in 1898, the club house is a striking yellow-stone building in pristine condition, with a colonial feel to it. Entry is restricted to members only. On the opposite side of the road is the magnificent Yacht Club, built in 1881. It was one of the earliest structures built along the harbour promenade. This 'off-limits' construction is known for its distinctive verandah with wooden frames on the sides.

A splendidly done English villa-type building, the Yacht Club has teakwood flooring and panels that make this structure stand apart from most buildings in the vicinity. Beside the Yacht Club House is the Royal Bombay Yacht Club Annexe and Residential Chambers that came up in 1898. It was designed by John

▲
Yacht Club

Adams and his friend, architect F.W. Stevens in Gothic style. F.W. Stevens was assisted by his son Charles, who ensured that the strictest engineering details were maintained. Hydraulic lifts, electric lights and fire services were integral to the building plan.

For a while in the 1950s and early 60s, the prestigious Tata Institute of Fundamental Research was housed in the Royal Yacht Club premises. In 1962, they shifted to the present location at the Navy Nagar campus in south Mumbai.

Taj Mahal Hotel and Taj Intercontinental

The Taj Mahal Hotel is synonymous with Mumbai. And the one name that immediately comes to mind is the enterprising Jamsetji Tata - industrialist and visionary, one of Mumbai's biggest benefactors of all time. Spurned when he was refused entry to the elitist Watson's on Esplanade, he vowed to build a bigger, far better five-star hotel that would overshadow and outshine the Watson's in splendour and style. He most definitely succeeded!

He went all out to ensure that the Taj was the best-equipped hotel with its own electric laundry, Turkish baths, post office, pharmacy and resident doctor. It was designed by a local firm of architects called Chambers, in a unique Byzantine manner. Tata himself conceived most of the design along with Raosaheb Sitaram Vaidya, who went on to become the Resident Engineer of Bombay. This hotel, with its great dome - 282 feet in height - makes a striking

►
The Taj Mahal Hotel

landmark for incoming ships to the harbour. However, the hotel's grand foyer and its lawns do not face the sea but look inward at the city. The Taj Mahal Hotel has grown in stature over the years and even a century later still remains Mumbai's most sought after five-star luxury hotel. The splendid Taj Ballroom was done in the Art Deco style by E.F. Messerschimdt. Its high-rise counterpart—The Taj Intercontinental—came up much later and perfectly complements its more historic cousin, despite the contrasting blend of the old and new architectural styles.

Gateway of India

At the end of the Apollo Pier, jutting into the harbour is the historic Gateway of India, Mumbai's most prominent landmark. Much before the present-day structure of the Gateway was built, it was a makeshift iron-shed with a curved roof. It stood as a vantage point to incoming ships as they neared the natural harbour off Mumbai's Apollo Bunder.

An aerial view of the Gateway promenade
▼

This temporary shed was built in the style of a Mongol tent and became a shelter for passengers in the early British era.

Just before King George V's visit to India in 1911, the iron shed was haphazardly replaced with a pavilion and hall made of white Plaster of Paris. The King and Queen departed from the same temporary structure on 10 January 1912. Soon after they left India's shores, Governor Sydenham initiated a scheme to commence work on a permanent structure.

This reclaimed frontage to the north of the Taj Mahal Hotel was meant to be an imposing stone-landing stage, unique in design. The inaugural stone was laid in 1913, and work began to level the promenade around the plaza. The impressive archway was eventually complete by 1927.

Designed by George Wittet, the Gateway was a cross between the Parisian Arc de Triomphe, a Moorish mansion and old Gujarati architecture. It comprises a main, large arch that reaches a maximum height of eighty-three feet, flanked by two smaller arches. The fretted framework above the arches is heavily influenced by the sixteenth century Gujarati architecture. Honey-coloured yellow basalt stone to build the Gateway came from Kharodi in Thane, while stone for the pierced stonework was brought from Gwalior. The Gateway Plaza has a fine equestrian statue of the Maratha king Chhatrapati Shivaji and an imposing statue of the philosopher Swami Vivekananda. Architect Wittet, had also proposed a grand avenue beside the Gateway that was never implemented.

A pleasant half hour launch ride transports you from the noisy metropolis to the quiet, architecturally invaluable island of Elephanta, known in ancient times as Gharapuri (fortress city). A series of seven magnificent rock-cut caves dedicated to Shiva date back to AD 4 to

DID YOU KNOW?

Towards the end of the seventeenth century, the **harbour of Bombay** was included in the logs of several ships, with precise instructions to avoid the dreaded Sunken Rock which was just off the coast near the Fort. As early as 1690, a map by Jacob Ward (one of the earliest maps to give an accurate picture of Bombay) showed the island of Bombay with Middle Ground, Cross Island, Sunken Rock, Oyster Rock, Butcher and Elephanta islands - all mentioned at accurate locations near the harbour!

AD 9 and these caves are located roughly at 250 feet above sea level. It became an English possession in 1774, before which it belonged to the Marathas. This site is today on the UNESCO World Heritage Site map and needs to be preserved for its rich, historic past.

The Victoria

Records mention that the Victoria first made its presence known on the city's streets way back in 1882 when an English merchant named Webber introduced it to the city's population. Till then, britzkas, omnibuses, clarences, buggies, palanquins, tillburys (all types of public carriages) and chariots were integral to the city's transport. In fact the Victoria traces its roots to the gharry. The gharry was a horse-driven carriage that formed part of Mumbai's road transport in the beginning of the nineteenth century.

A modified version of it was called the Victoria. Today, these horse carriages are dying a slow death. Most of them are seen plying near the Gateway Plaza catering to the ever-curious tourist. Its garish rexene upholstery and equally eye-catching silver exteriors make them a huge draw. Hefty rates for a ride down the promenade ensure that these remnants of the Raj survive, for how long, who knows…

The lighthouses off the Mumbai harbour

The port and harbour along with its approaches are well illuminated. The three main entrance lights are Prongs Lighthouse to the north, Kennery Lighthouse to the south and the unattended Floating Light Vessel moored in forty feet at low water, in the entrance to the harbour fairway.

Of these, Kennery is situated on an island by the same name, which was once the

stronghold of the Angres - Maratha sea admirals, known for their sharp acumen in fighting sea battles in the sixteenth and seventeenth centuries. The Prongs Lighthouse marks a reef that runs southward from Colaba Point and is surrounded by reefs and dangerous ground extending up to a mile from it. It was the city's earliest lighthouse, built in 1875, and can be reached on foot from the southern tip of Colaba at low tide in spring. The Floating Light Vessel exhibits its light from a masthead thirty-two feet above the water. The light is visible in clear weather from a distance of eleven miles! Another important light for the harbour is the unattended Sunk Rock Lighthouse. It was built on a patch of rock, two miles east-north-east of Prongs Lighthouse. The other subsidiary lights of the Harbour are the Dolphin Rock Light, Middle Ground Island and Tucker Beacon Light.

Apollo Bunder promenade

It was the Apollo Reclamation project, completed in 1869 that made way for the development and construction of buildings like the Taj Mahal Hotel, Yacht Club premises and much later the Gateway of India, over the next three or four decades. It also led to the creation of residential buildings between the Apollo Bunder promenade all the way up to Colaba

►

Dawn by the Apollo Bunder Promenade

Causeway. The line of colonial style buildings along the Prem Ramchandani Marg near the Taj Mahal Hotel looks like an intact oil canvas from Mumbai's past. This promenade by the Gateway was developed between 1941 and 1965 and has remained one of the most beautiful sights near the harbour. Seemingly untouched by the commercial air of its many affluent neighbours, these buildings that came up in the early and mid-1900s are reminiscent of a colonial history.

Beautiful English villas and residences with private porches and driveways, cream and lime coated exteriors complementing the stiff sea breeze, impressive arches and leafy pavements transport one to a different era altogether. What with names like The Anchorage, Belha Court, Manor Haven, Villar Velle, the picture is complete for the perfect English seaside suburb. One noteworthy mention is Evelyn House, owned by the Port Trust, which has been renovated and modernised from within and outside—an ideal example of the restoration carried out along this heritage promenade. The Northcote Hospital is another interesting reminder from the days of the Raj. Strand Hotel, Sea Palace, Hotel Prosser's, Shelley's Hotel and the Gateway Hotel add to the colonial charm of this sea facing promenade.

The Radio Club

The Radio Club was established on a sea facing site near the Grants Buildings at the edge of the Apollo Bunder promenade, where Prem Ramchandani Marg meets with Minoo Desai Road. It goes back a long way to the time when the Bombay Radio Club inaugurated a radio service in June 1924 on a Marconi transmitter - the first of its kind in western India. Technically, the Bombay radio

The Radio Club

station was the same as the London 2LO station. It cost nearly Rs. 2 lakhs to erect and the estimated cost of running and maintaining each was Rs. 1.8 lakhs per annum.

On 23 July 1927, the Indian Broadcasting Company was inaugurated at Radio House, Apollo Bunder and regular broadcasting commenced thereafter. This service was set up on an experimental basis in Bombay and Calcutta simultaneously, based on an agreement between the Government of India and a private company, called the Indian Broadcasting Company Ltd. Its broadcasting studio was connected by a P&T line to a transmitter located at Worli. At that time, the acoustics of the studios, like hanging of coloured drapes, created a huge interest among the Indian press. This studio became the Mecca of Bombay's musicians till the late 1920s. Today, the club has evolved into one of the city's premier residential clubhouses with excellent clubhouse facilities to its members.

DETOUR: Henry Street - Mereweather Road - Tullock Road

Walk down the Taj Mahal Hotel's sea-facing façade, take the first turn to your right and stroll into Henry Street. It will introduce you to another world - of quieter lanes and curious onlookers, of buildings and establishments that still survive from a forgotten time. An odd Arab here, a fez cap there and the entire street culture is one of unmistakable Middle-Eastern charm.

Parallel to the impressive Taj Mahal Hotel is Mereweather Road. This road, steeped in history, might go unnoticed, largely due to the overpowering presence of Jamsetji Tata's most famous creation in the background. Tiny curio shops display fascinating ware from all over India to interest the die-hard art collector. Emporiums and carpet shops are seen here by the dozen. Trendy restaurants, boutiques, salons and lounge bars make unusual neighbours for the crumbling colonial structures, like the Carlton Hotel and Devidas Mansion. Some of the older businesses like Radiant Tailors and Hotel Diplomat remain intact. The Red Shield House, of the Salvation Army at the junction of BEST Marg and Mereweather Road is another impressive structure, with its bright red and cream coloured exterior - like a breath of fresh air among the many buildings which are in a sorry state of ruin.

The Florence House and Roosevelt House are some of the Grade-III type heritage structures along Mereweather Road to display trappings of colonial style architecture. Most of the buildings along this road display an arcade-like pattern, while some are made in the newer Art Deco style of architecture that Mumbai adopted for many of its buildings in the 1930s. The most famous address on Tullock Road (that runs parallel to Mereweather Road) is undoubtedly, Bade Miya. This eatery, which over fifty years old, is legendary in the city and is a must-stop for all food lovers. Succulent kebabs, lip-smacking stuffed baida parathas and heavenly chicken tikka rolls are dished out to the city's foodies till as late as 3 am! In fact, the aroma of tandoori food pervades the air and tempts the visitor several streets ahead. A favourite hangout among the city's disco-hoppers as well as its dock labourers, no other roadside eatery can boast of being such a great leveller. Typical of the city's cosmopolitan fabric...

ಬಂಧ

The Red Shield House building
▼

A Victorian Ensemble: The City's Most Famous Building Landscape

(National Gallery of Modern Art - University Buildings - Metro Cinema)

*O*pen green spaces, clubhouses, art galleries, commanding institutes of learning, sprawling campuses, an imposing clock tower, Venetian-Gothic buildings - these sights conjure images of a laid-back English town. Well, not quite. In the very heart of Mumbai's chaos, is a slice of the city at its most scenic, stimulating best. The gallery, the science institute and the university will stir the senses of the scholar, the researcher or the art lover. The open spaces of the maidan will tempt the daydreamer to fix a permanent gaze on a most spectacular skyline that surrounds him on every side, the sports lover can relive the aura of the British Raj, rugby and cricket, over a leisurely cuppa. And finally, for the film lover, the once resplendent environs of the Metro Cinema should be a perfect ending point. So, take that invigorating stroll, Mumbai style...

APPROXIMATE DISTANCE
2 kilometres

APPROACH/PARKING
You can start by boarding any Colaba-bound BEST bus from either Churchgate or Chhatrapati Shivaji Terminus and alight at the stop near the Museum. Other options include hailing a taxi from either of the two railway terminuses. The minimum fare is all you need to dole out to reach the starting point of the walk-The National Gallery of Modern Art. Parking is available at the Kala Ghoda circle, barely a minute away from the gallery. It would help if you start early to manage some parking space in this bustling circle.

PLACES OF INTEREST

- National Gallery of Modern Art
- St. Anne's High School
- YWCA International Guest House
- Amerchand Mansion
- Oval Maidan
- Art Deco buildings overlooking the Oval Maidan
- Indian Institute of Science
- Civil and Sessions Court
- University Buildings
- Rajabai Clock Tower
- Bombay High Court
- Public Works Department Building
- Central Telegraph Office
- Bhika Behram Well
- Bombay Gymkhana
- Row of sports and musical goods stores
- Metro Cinema complex

THE WALK

Beginning the walk amidst the culturally-inspired surroundings of the Kala Ghoda Art District is most ideal for the heritage and arts enthusiast. Loaded with interesting sights and sounds throughout, the walk covers a wide spectrum of the old and new worlds. It commences within the hallowed walls of the National Gallery of Modern Art, Mumbai's showcase of rich Indian art and culture.

National Gallery of Modern Art

The National Gallery of Modern Art was built on the curve where Mahatma Gandhi Road meets Madam Cama Road, with the Wellington Junction facing it at a distance. The interior of the Sir Cowasjee Jehangir Hall was remodelled later to accommodate the NGMA. This conversion was carried out by the PWD (Public Works Department), according to the designs of Delhi-based architect Romi Khosla. Thankfully, the designs were well-executed and what resulted was a fine blend of architectural styles, without marring the impressive heritage landscape in the vicinity.

It remains the only art gallery in India to be fully administered by the Indian government. The gallery was inaugurated on 29 March 1954 and displays the gradual evolution of Indian art since 1857, through the colonial years and post-Independence. NGMA has played a crucial and highly supportive role for Indian art, especially with the case of modern Indian artists. The prestigious Jehangir Nicholson Art Gallery is also housed inside the NGMA. It has a splendid collection of modern Indian art displayed in rotation with special exhibitions.

The National Gallery of Modern Art
▼

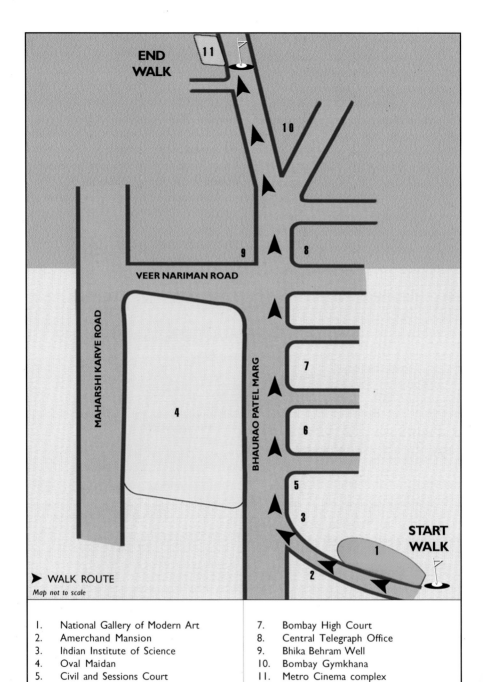

END WALK

11

10

9

8

VEER NARIMAN ROAD

MAHARSHI KARVE ROAD

BHAURAO PATEL MARG

4

7

6

5

3

2

1

START WALK

▶ WALK ROUTE

Map not to scale

1.	National Gallery of Modern Art	7.	Bombay High Court
2.	Amerchand Mansion	8.	Central Telegraph Office
3.	Indian Institute of Science	9.	Bhika Behram Well
4.	Oval Maidan	10.	Bombay Gymkhana
5.	Civil and Sessions Court	11.	Metro Cinema complex
6.	University Buildings and Rajabai Clock Tower		

St. Anne's High School for Girls (Convent of Jesus and Mary)

On the opposite side of Madam Cama Road is one of the city's premier schools for girls - St. Anne's High School. The structure housing this premier school is a Grade-III heritage building, grey dour-looking old stone building with typical arches reflecting Gothic influence throughout the outer façade.

YWCA International Guest House

Beside it, is the hugely popular YWCA Guesthouse, set up in the 1920s. Easily one of the more impressive buildings along this stretch, its quaint, old-world charm immediately grabs your attention. It provides highly economical, comfortable and convenient accommodation for unmarried young women - students as well as working women. Such is its stock and standing that this women's guesthouse remains one of the most sought-after addresses for new entrants to the city and applicants remain on its waiting list for months together.

Amerchand Mansion

Next door is the impressive commercial building that also came up in the early twentieth century. The ground-floor houses a plush restaurant, business establishments, travel agencies and airline offices, while some of the upper levels are residential premises. A typical old-fashioned elevator, wooden interiors and a spacious entrance shows that the building is still trapped in another era altogether. The brick-red outer façade of this building however, gives it a certain freshness, warmth and colour, in complete contrast to the otherwise more sedate exteriors of its neighbours along this road.

History of the Esplanade and its surroundings

As one takes a turn for the Karmveer Bhaurao Patil Road, the vastness of space almost takes you by surprise. You face the sprawling Oval Maidan. But first, a little history about this part before we proceed any further.

By 1753, the area around Fort was so congested that all the structures around Fort (including the Oval Maidan) were bought by the East India Company and demolished. The process was quickened because sometime in the 1770s, the British feared an attack by the French from the Arabian Sea. So the panic-struck Company cleared and levelled an expansive semi-circular stretch near the Bombay Fort walls and called it the Esplanade. This stretch was originally reserved as a

DID YOU KNOW?

It was during the city's first Municipal Commissioner Arthur Crawford's tenure that wide avenues were constructed through the Esplanade, whereby the 'maidan' was divided into four major sections - **Cooperage, Oval Maidan, Cross Maidan** and **Azad Maidan**.

British officers on duty at the Fort often played cricket at the northern end of the Esplanade, much to the interest of the local Indian population.

compulsory open space to provide a clear range of fire from the Fort walls. Its northern end stretched up to Lohar Chawl while the southern end lay beyond present-day Cooperage to where the Colaba Railway Station once stood. In fact, until the nineteenth century, its parametres extended 400 yards from the ramparts to the edge of the sea. By 1804, it was increased to 800 yards and later to 1000 yards to ensure a larger open space.

Post-1864, after Governor Bartle Frere ordered the demolition of the Fort walls to decongest the city, the western edge of the Fort area saw several public buildings appear on the map. These buildings (High Court, University Buildings, Old Secretariat) positioned themselves along the edge of the street with the Esplanade (today's Oval and Cross Maidans) in the forefront. The vacant land available here was the main reason for this new development.

A magnificent ensemble of Victorian-styled buildings changed the city landscape forever. Today, these buildings represent some of the most prominent landmarks of Mumbai and together they have transformed Mumbai's skyline along its western edge to give it a completely new identity. The high quality and superior architectural style was due to the availability of solid local stone near the city and skilled craftsmen who emerged from the newly established Bombay School of Art. Most of these buildings came

Oval Maidan
▼

up between 1865-74 and they collectively rank among the most splendid, finest examples of architecture in British India. This entire group has been repeatedly acclaimed as the 'finest Victorian ensemble of the world.' Some of them are mentioned later in this chapter.

Oval Maidan

Part of the sprawling open space called the Esplanade, the Oval Maidan became a separate landmass much later, in the twentieth century. It was a time when the city's roads were laid out, especially to connect the Fort area and Flora Fountain square with the western foreshore overlooking the Arabian Sea near present-day Churchgate Railway Station. This required that the Esplanade to be split into several smaller partitions-Cooperage, Oval Maidan, Cross Maidan and Azad Maidan, and this is what is left of the grand Esplanade. The Oval Maidan derived its name from the shape it acquired after the divisions took place. The Oval lay beyond the walls and battlements of the old Fort. It was a huge draw among residents from the Fort area who flocked to this open space, which enjoyed an unobstructed view of the sea at the turn of the twentieth century until the 1930s. The maidan was also a place of entertainment where bands would play in the evenings for the European settlers of the city. The city's more affluent residents could be seen enjoying horse carriage rides or drives in their Ford motor cars on this open stretch.

Today, the maidan is in better shape than even a decade ago. It has managed to recapture the flavour of the past with its 185 palms on the fringes and 90,000 sq. ft of fencing. The only major change made was the creation of a walking track to replace the defunct riding-cum-walking track. Minimal changes were allowed with a view to prolonging the life of the precinct. It was an under-utilised scrub land with no heritage status when former cricketer Dilip Vengsarkar was leased the cricket pitch in 1994 to train young aspiring cricketers. He founded the Elf-Vengsarkar Cricket Academy on the north side of the ground. The academy has been doing a commendable job of training youngsters, a huge per cent of whom play for Mumbai. The south side of the Oval is open to the public. On any given evening, athletes, joggers and football teams can be seen jostling for that bit of extra legroom on one of the city's last surviving open spaces.

Art Deco buildings can be spotted lining the entire stretch opposite the Oval Maidan
▼

Art Deco buildings overlooking Oval Maidan

In the 1930s, many of the city's buildings were hugely influenced by the wave of Art Deco architecture that was sweeping across Europe and North America. This 'pop-art' style added a completely different dimension to the city's skyline with its colourful, geometric exteriors, broad balconies in all sizes and so on. Several buildings along the the west, facing the Oval Maidan, up to the Eros Cinema on the north, were built in this style. Old-time residents of these buildings swear that back in the 1940s and 50s, this stretch was almost like a piece of Miami right here in Mumbai! With real estate here touching the roof, these residential buildings remain one of the most sought-after areas. After all, who would forfeit boasting of one of the city's best views from their balconies!

▲

The Indian Institute of Science is recognisable for its curved building design

And now for a look at some of the most important educational and public establishments that came up in the city facing the Oval Maidan on the former Esplanade Road (now Karmveer Bhaurao Patel Road).

Indian Institute of Science

Running almost parallel to the Oval Maidan, is the Institute of Science, formerly known as the Royal Institute of Science. Built in the Renaissance revivalist style at the very start of the Bhaurao Karmveer Road, this institute is worth several trips for the curious-minded. Just stepping inside this temple of learning and its spacious interiors nearly overwhelm the visitor. One is greeted by a huge, imposing white marble

The open spiral staircase is an inspiring work of architecture in the University building complex

statue of Governor Sydenham, who was responsible to a great extent for the setting up of this prestigious institute dedicated to the cause of science in the city. Architect George Wittet designed the Institute and used single-coloured yellow basalt stone throughout its exteriors. The building exhibits a predominantly European style. It was opened in 1920 and designed as a visual extension of the row of Gothic buildings along Esplanade Road.

Civil and Sessions Court

Next door to the imposing institute is the Civil and Sessions Court. This magnificent structure was once home to the old Bombay Government Secretariat. The building is a 143 metre (470 feet) tall structure with two wings, in the Venetian Gothic style. It was designed and built by the architect Colonel Henry Wilkins between 1865-74. The exterior carvings are the handiwork of Indian artists. The structure is a continuation of the series of Gothic revival buildings that were built at the edge of the Esplanade when the old Fort walls were pulled down.

A massive fifty-two metre (170 feet) tower that rises over a twenty-seven metre (ninety feet) window admits light onto the inner staircase. The building also displays a finely arcaded porch. Today, this grand piece of architecture is partially obscured by a row of temporary police structures. The architecture of this once splendid construction may have dulled due to neglect.

University Buildings

Across A.S. D'Mello Road from the Old Secretariat are two old, beautiful, and important buildings belonging to Mumbai University (established in 1857). They were designed in England by Sir George Gilbert Scott, who had already given the world the Gothic extravaganza of London's St. Pancras railway station. Founded in the same year, it was one of the earliest universities in the country, along with the Calcutta and Madras Universities, to be established in British India. Some of the finest buildings within its complex include the Senate Hall, the University Library and the Rajabai Clock Tower.

Sir Scott was the only recognised and distinguished British architect in his time to contribute towards the city's architecture. The University library as well as the clock tower was funded by banker and 'cotton king' Premchand Roychand. In all, he donated over four lakh rupees for the building of the University and the clock tower. The University Hall, is named after Roychand for his generous contributions. They were based on a French decorative style reminiscent of the fifteenth century. Funded by the Parsi philanthropist Cowasjee 'Readymoney' Jehangir, the Convocation Hall greatly resembles a church. Above its entrance, a massive, circular stained-glass window depicts a wheel with spokes of

Greek pilasters that separate the twelve signs of the zodiac. One of the most impressive designs is that of the open spiral staircases, measuring thirty-two metres long, thirteen metres wide and nineteen metres high all the way to the apex of the ceiling. A statue of Sir Cowasjee stands at the entrance. Sir Pherozeshah Mehta laid the foundation stone for the Convocation Hall of the University as well as the adjacent Rajabai Clock Tower.

Rajabai Clock Tower

The Venetian-Gothic style University Library and Rajabai Clock Tower were also designed by Sir Gilbert Scott. The library within the tower is a long, low room with traces of carving. This resplendent clock tower, part of the library, measures 230 feet high and remained the tallest structure within the city limits through the late 1900s till the mid-twentieth century. Funded by 'cotton king' Sir Premchand Roychand, the splendid structure was named after his mother. Completed in 1878, the tower is octagonal

►
A closer view of the Rajabai Tower

DID YOU KNOW?

Premchand Roychand made a massive fortune because of the speculative frenzy as a result of the Bombay cotton boom in the early 1860s. He was one of the city's most prominent merchants to have benefitted from this mania. The main reason behind this sudden demand for cotton occurred because of the US Civil War that prevented American cotton from reaching the British market. India was the natural choice to turn to for cotton.

and lantern-shaped, topped by a spire. Twenty carved figures in the niches represent different castes of western India. They measure 8 feet in height and are created in Porbander stone. In fact, the tower is said to be modelled on Giotto's campanile in Florence, Italy. These impeccable figures were executed by students from the Sir JJ School of Art. The fourth floor houses the grand clock, which until 1931, chimed tunes, such as, 'Rule Britannia,' 'God Save The Queen', 'Home Sweet Home' along with hymns on Sundays and other favourites on weekdays.

▲

Several stalwarts of the Indian freedom struggle, including Dr. BR Ambedkar, practiced law at the Bombay High Court

Bombay High Court

Next in line is situated the imposing white-pinnacled and blue-basalt structure that cannot be missed by anyone passing by this stretch of Victorian-inspired buildings. Designed by General James A. Fuller of the Royal Engineers in a typical English style, the High Court is a towering presence along the former

Esplanade Road at 169 metres (roughly 562 feet) with its soaring fifty-three metre high tower. It was completed in 1878, the same year as the University Library and Convocation Hall. However, this public building opened in 1879. One is greeted at the entrance with a large arched porch, flanked by two octagonal thirty-six metre high towers whose white Porbander stone pinnacles are crowned with the statues of Justice and Mercy.

The interiors are resplendent and represent a quiet dignity - you come across dark, polished teak ceilings with an impressive centrepiece and an Italian mosaic floor. The pillared galleries have interesting carvings on them - apes at play, a half-blind ape holding aloft the scales of justice, a fox wearing a barrister's bands, and a pig and tiger engaged in a fight. Most of this amusing ornamentation was the work of Indian stone masons.

Public Works Department Building

Next to the High Court, is the Public Works Department building on Veer Nariman Road. It was completed by 1872, and like many buildings in the vicinity, was made of grey stone without giving too much attention to aesthetics in its design and layout. The exterior and interior of the building reflect the purely functional nature of this building. Till today, this Grade-I heritage site is almost lost among the grandeur and brilliance of its more prominent neighbours.

Ironically, it is to the PWD that credit must go for hiring architects who were behind the designs for several of these public utility buildings. This department began to hire professionals trained in architecture instead of military engineers to design this ensemble of buildings and were therefore responsible for the fine range of buildings along Esplanade Road.

Central Telegraph Office

Another Grade-I heritage structure, it was completed in 1874 and stood opposite the PWD Building on Veer Nariman Road. This public building displayed a bright Romanesque façade made of coarse rubble stone from Kurla and columns of blue basalt stone in its heyday. It was built from the designs of J. Trubshawe and W. Paris, architects to the Government. This building previously housed the General Post Office until it shifted to its present site near the Central Railway terminus. Alas, today the picture has changed for the worse, with the building in desperate need for restoration. A sorry picture since its glory days. This structure is currently undergoing restoration work.

Bhikha Behram Well

After crossing the crowded traffic signal, the Bhika Behram Well is our next stop. At one end of the Cross Maidan, this is one of the most sacred places of worship for the Zoroastrian community in the city. Also known as the 'Bhika Behram-no-kuvo', it is a freshwater well built in 1725. The striking fact about this well is that it always has fresh water despite its proximity to the sea. During the Zoroastrian month of 'Aran,' when the divinity of water is worshipped, this well is lined with oil lamps, transforming it into a breathtakingly beautiful site.

The site has an interesting history. Bhikaji Behramji came from Broach (in Gujarat) to Bombay in 1715. He was arrested and imprisoned by the Marathas, who mistook him for a Muslim. It was only after he showed them his sacred vest (sudreh) and cord (kusti) that he was released. He had earlier vowed that if set free he would build a well for his community and he kept his word. The well and its canopy were named after him ten years later. In fact, in its

▲

Above: The Bombay Gymkhana remains one of the last surviving institutions that still seems struck in a bygone era

early days, during high tide sea water would lap its outer perimetre, yet the water inside was always fresh water. Today, it is a heritage site and still continues to yield abundant water throughout the year.

Further down from this Parsi place of worship you come across sights like the Videsh Sanchar Nigam Limited building, a towering modern structure. Ahead is the very popular Fashion Street - the redoubtable Mecca for affordable clothes and accessories. Opposite this half-mile stretch is one of the most recognisable sites from the British Raj - the Bombay Gymkhana, the status symbol for the well-heeled Mumbaiite.

Bombay Gymkhana

The Bombay Gymkhana was established in 1875, as the city's premier centre for the activities of several sporting clubs. Claude Batley, a former principal at the Sir JJ School of Art designed this sprawling gymkhana house. The striking green and yellow structure gives the feel of a British club with all the trappings

of a bygone era.

The club was especially formed for rugby in 1875 by the British. Today, Bombay Gymkhana is the premier rugby institution in the country - best reflected by the fact that a majority of its players are in the twenty-four-member Indian team. This 'By Invitation Only' club has tennis and squash courts, enclosed grounds that double up for cricket and rugby and a swimming pool.

Indians were admitted as members of the Bombay Gymkhana only after 1947. In December 1933, the Gymkhana was the venue for the first ever cricket Test played in Mumbai. The match was between India and a touring English side led by Douglas Jardine. India was led by 'Colonel' CK Nayadu. The Indian side lost the Test by nine wickets. Lala Amarnath became the first Indian to score a century, and that too on his debut against Jardine's England team at the Bombay Gymkhana in 1933-34.

The NCC Directorate and the 111 Movement Service Area, which constitute a part of the Indian Armed Forces establishment, is what meets the eye, immediately where Fashion Street ends. The stark, grey-coloured building resembles a typical military structure with a complete 'no-frills' approach.

Row of music and sports good stores

Immediately after moving past the military establishment, the landscape becomes more commercial and chaotic as one nears the Dhobi Talao traffic signal. Sports goods stores jostle for space with others selling musical instruments, trophies, medallions and shields. This area prides itself for being home to some of the city's oldest establishments catering to the requirements of sports and music lovers. The more popular among them include Marques & Sons Music Salon, Action (established in 1938) and Caxton Sports Stores and Jhaveri Bros. The nondescript-looking Jhaveri Bros has achieved near legend-like status since it was set up in 1914. It is one of the most sought-after stores to make trophies, mementos, shields and other citations in various metals and alloys.

Metro Cinema complex

Adjacent to these commercial establishments is the sprawling Metro Cinema complex that was opened to the public in 1938, several months after Eros began public screenings, with the *Broadway Melody of 1938*. The theatre was entirely developed by American entertainment giant Metro-Goldwyn-Mayer. The cinema complex was designed by MGM and the well-known Bombay architectural firm of Ditchburn & Mistri. Street-level shops, six levels of offices and a parking lot gave Metro much to boast about. Interestingly, the cinema was built in such a way that it remained isolated from the rest of the building by a corner tower and a parking lot. This upmarket cinema was introduced in the city's newspapers as the cinema, 'Where The Lion Roars'!

The building was made of reinforced

DID YOU KNOW?

Metro Cinema was acquired by the Metro Goldwyn Corporation in 1936 on a lease for 999 years at a nominal ground rent of Re. 1 per annum! The site for the cinema, a former stable for the Royal Air Force, was chosen at the pivotal Dhobi Talao junction where six roads converged.

concrete around a tower at a public and crowded corner and served as a landmark. It was a dividing point between the Indian township and the wealthy European district. Some of its biggest draws were the ever-popular soda fountain, teak covered columns, white marbled floors and two fifteen-feet high aluminium and cut-glass chandeliers.

The lobby had all the trappings of a swanky cinema—bright American fabrics and interiors, furniture by Wimbridge & Co, exposed metal doors and aluminium railings imported from America and two-storey high steel-framed windows! The 1,500-seater cinema displayed a mix of bright Art Deco murals and designs from Hindu epics within and outside the lobby, designed by professors from the Sir JJ School of Art and executed by its students. Until Independence, the cinema openly showed social differences among its benefactors, with separate balcony seating arrangements for the 'upper classes.'

Sadly, the grand cinema building will make way for its new look as a multiplex. With it, the city will lose an integral part of its history and heritage. Thus, another landmark of this area's rich architecture has fallen to the sharks of commercialisation.

৯০৫৪

Chronicles Of Colaba Causeway: Rediscovering Colaba and Its Treasures

(Museum - Sassoon Docks - INHS Asvini)

*V*isualise this. A sleepy fishing hamlet called Kolvan (or Kola-bhat) facing the Arabian Sea. Its inhabitants, the Koli fisherfolk, carry on with their daily chores, unaware of the outside world. Flash forward several centuries and you have this swanky fashion district, big city lights and speeding cars whizzing past fair-skinned bagpackers, as they wrestle their way through crowds in search of rare artefacts along the inner lanes of the causeway. But of course, we are talking of Colaba. The Kolis have almost disappeared from their stronghold, on their villages now stand concrete jungles and what was once a secluded British cantonment that prohibited ordinary citizens from taking residence is now a shopping paradise, with a pulsating nightlife. To say that this coconut grove on Mumbai's southernmost tip underwent a sea change would be stating the obvious. With such an intriguing past and a vibrant character, it's only natural to explore this area. The history—seen and unseen—will keep you company on this walk.

APPROXIMATE DISTANCE
4.5 kilometres

APPROACH/PARKING
If you are bringing along your private vehicle, then parking at the Kala Ghoda circle is ideal as it's the closest from the start of your walk. If you prefer public transport, you may alight at either the Churchgate or Chhatrapati Shivaji (Victoria) Terminus and board a BEST bus or hail a taxi to reach the Museum.

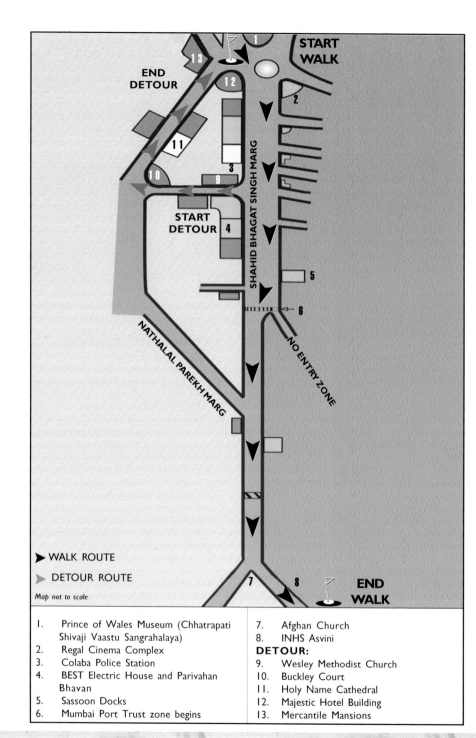

1.	Prince of Wales Museum (Chhatrapati Shivaji Vaastu Sangrahalaya)	7.	Afghan Church
2.	Regal Cinema Complex	8.	INHS Asvini
3.	Colaba Police Station	**DETOUR:**	
4.	BEST Electric House and Parivahan Bhavan	9.	Wesley Methodist Church
5.	Sassoon Docks	10.	Buckley Court
6.	Mumbai Port Trust zone begins	11.	Holy Name Cathedral
		12.	Majestic Hotel Building
		13.	Mercantile Mansions

PLACES OF INTEREST

- Prince of Wales Museum (Chhatrapati Shivaji Vaastu Sangrahalaya)
- Regal Cinema Complex
- Café Mondegar, Café Leopold, Piccadilly Restaurant and Café Churchill
- Colaba Police Station
- BEST Electric House & Parivahan Bhavan
- Cusrow Baug
- Strand Cinema
- Kailas Parbat Restaurant
- Sassoon Docks
- Bombay Baptist Church and RC Church
- Colaba Defence Station
- Afghan Church
- INHS Asvini

DETOUR

- Wesley Methodist Church
- Buckley Court
- Holy Name Cathedral
- YMCA and CBI House
- Majestic Hotel Building
- Mercantile Mansions

THE WALK

Before we begin this walk, devoted to Colaba, it's worthwhile to go back in time to document why Colaba is so integral to the evolution of this city. Steeped in history, it made up one of the original seven islands. According to records dating back to 1675, Governor Gerald Aungier took control of Colaba and, to its north, the Old Woman's Island, from the Portuguese. In 1743, it was leased to a wealthy British called Richard Broughton at Rs. 200 per annum! The lease was renewed in 1764. In time, this area developed into an important British cantonment. Yet there was a regular passage of people from the main island to these southern islands. Eventually, a causeway was built in 1838 due to public pressure and to prevent huge boating accidents. Colaba became the first island that was connected to the main island by the city's first causeway. A solid pathway with a footpath protecting the elevated road was built. This was a milestone that opened up new land to develop this region into a busy mercantile centre.

The causeway was further widened in 1861, and again in 1863, because of the burgeoning population. By 1872, Colaba became a separate ward of the Municipality. Since then, this picturesque causeway and its surroundings have emerged as a blend of the old and new, an eclectic mix of smoky cafés, vibrant restaurants, streetside bazaars, trendy boutiques and lifestyle stores, places of worship and upmarket residences.

This walk begins at Prince of Wales Museum, arguably one of our most prized possessions and staunch guardian of the city's immeasurable treasures.

Prince of Wales Museum (renamed Chhatrapati Shivaji Vaastu Sangrahalaya)

This Moorish-styled building may have weathered with time, but once inside, you're overwhelmed by its wealth. Priceless art, archaeology and natural history collections can be found here. Its foundation stone was laid by the Prince of Wales (later King George V) on his visit to the city, in 1905. The building, decorated in blue and yellow basalt, has three main sections: Art, Archaeology and Natural History. Two more sections were added later - Forestry and Geology. The museum was designed by George Wittet, who also designed the Gateway of India, Institute of Science, KEM Hospital and laid out the Ballard Estate sub-precinct.

It was completed in 1923 to commemorate the visit of the Prince of Wales in the same year. It even served as a hospital during World War I. The structure bears a striking resemblance to the Gol Gumbaz of Bijapur. The crescent-shaped museum, built in the Indo-Saracenic style had huge Indian influences in its architecture - from Rajput jharokas, brackets inspired by Hindu temples and semi-open verandahs.

Sir Ratan Tata's collections from the Dutch, British, French and Italian schools adorn the Art section. Oriental arms, spectacular exhibits of jade, fine china, Indian brass, silver as well as Indian and Persian carpets are seen here. The Archaeological section is divided into Brahmanical, Jain, prehistoric and foreign antiques and a Buddhist section. The Natural History section

DID YOU KNOW?

Old Woman's Island was the smaller island to the north of Colaba. Some believe it to be the English corruption of 'Al-Omani', given by Arab seafarers because of deep-sea fishermen who came here from the Sea of Oman. Other versions obtained ranged from a rigidly carved red-smeared goddess, a venerable Portuguese dame, a wrinkled, fate-reading fisherwoman. Some city historians maintain that British sailors may have twisted the term from the Portuguese 'Kolvan' after the Koli hamlet. They dropped the initial 'K' and changed it to 'Olman' or 'Old Woman's Island'. Locally, the high ground within the eastern side of the Colaba bazaar once formed the island's summit. Its common name was Lower Colaba and comprised that part of Colaba closest to the city.

has vast contributions from the nearby Bombay Natural History Society (BNHS, started in 1883). Overall, the experience is invigorating for both the tourist and curious Mumbaiite.

Regal Cinema complex

Proceed past the Wellington Fountain to be greeted by the imposing Art Deco complex housing the Regal cinema. Renowned city architect F.W. Stevens' son Charles designed it using reinforced cement concrete, the first of its kind at the time. He spearheaded the Art Deco style of building design and its influence here is obvious. The famous Cubism exponent, Karl Schara, also had a hand in its ultra-modernist interiors. Built as the city's

first exclusive theatre for films, it augured the arrival of Art Deco in India. The idea to build this theatre came from Parsi entrepreneur Framji Sidhwa who bought the site to build, 'the best cinema East of Suez.' The 1,200-seater was India's largest, cooled by India's first ever air-conditioning system. The sixty-five feet long steel balcony provided for unobstructed seating and was done by Tata Iron & Steel Company (Jamshedpur). The auditorium structure covered India's first underground car park.

Governor of Bombay, Frederick Sykes, formally opened the cinema and its first show on 14 October 1933 was the Laurel and Hardy flick, *The Devil's Brother*. The theatre mostly screened American films because of Sidhwa's contract with MGM. In those times, seasonal bookings meant for weekend shows (for balcony seating) were quick sell-outs. Today, the interiors are neglected, its sheen has faded and Regal may be falling out of favour due to the multiplex

◄ *Regal Cinema*

A typical evening at Café Leopold
▼

> The Governor of Bombay, Frederick Sykes, formerly opened the cinema and its first show on 14 October 1933 was the Laurel and Hardy flick, *The Devil's Brother*

boom. Yet loyal patrons throng the city's oldest exclusive theatre out of sheer sentimental value.

Café Mondegar, Café Leopold, Picadilly Restaurant and Café Churchill

These cafes represent the very soul of Colaba Causeway. From English-styled fish 'n' chips to Lebanese shawarma, they serve it all. Buzzing with tourists from all over the globe as well as grungy-looking city collegians, these restaurants situated along Shahid Bhagat Singh Marg are the ideal hangouts for a slice of some

laidback ambience. The walls of Café Mondegar, (affectionately called 'Mondeez' by regulars) are adorned with Mario Miranda's caricatures reflecting city life - adding a local feel to the place. The jukebox plays a mix of retro, grunge, pop and disco and no one from the beer guzzler to the European bagpacker seem to mind the limited legroom and din.

Step outside Café Mondegar and two places immediately grab your attention: Shankar Book Stall, and the neighbouring jewellery store. Over fifty-years-old, and as famous as the café itself, the tiny bookstore is a must for the first-timer to the city, offering a range of guidebooks, maps, picture postcards and the like, besides an assortment of fiction, cookery and art books. Its immediate neighbour, Happy Stores, established in 1954, is a haven for those with a craving for junk jewellery and accessories. Like a bottomless pit, trinkets, pendants, bracelets and earrings seem to appear from nowhere as the owner tries to impress the interested customer with some truly fascinating wares from his collection.

Café Leopold is in the next block. This open house café gives a slight whiff of the Parisian café to Mumbaiites. Started in 1871, it's a landmark and big favourite among foreign tourists staying at the many lodges and hotels in Colaba. Its affordable menu and relaxed ambience draw in crowds till midnight. On the upper level is the pub 'Leo's Square', choc-a-bloc every day of the week and a huge draw for its peppy music and upbeat atmosphere. Opposite Leopold's are the smoky, almost forgotten Olympia Coffee House and Stores and the stark-looking Otis Building. Both constructions appear to have been witness to Colaba's metamorphosis.

Further ahead are the Picadilly Restaurant, opposite the Wesley Methodist Church and Café Churchill, opposite Cusrow Baug. Both have a typical café-like ambience, though they are less chaotic than the cafés described earlier. While Picadilly offers an interesting mix of Lebanese and Iranian fare, Churchill is a godsend for the Italian foodie, especially pastas and lasagna, not to forget, its well-cooked steaks and delightful desserts.

While on this restaurant crawl, you come across bylanes like Mahakavi Bhushan Marg, Nowroji Ferdunji Street and Mandlik Road. Each is filled with handicraft stores, art galleries and showrooms selling wares at exorbitant prices, boutiques and rare artefacts stores stocked with goods smuggled or imported from the Middle East. Interesting additions include stalls selling precious and semi-precious stones. Buying these wares is entirely at one's own risk.

Colaba Police Station

Further ahead from the Delhi Durbar restaurant is the historic Colaba Police Station. Believed to be one of the city's earliest police stations, it still functions from its original site. The structure came up in 1906 and is today included as a Grade-II heritage structure. It exhibits the typical grey-stone construction used in many public buildings of the area. Step inside this complex and it still manages to retain a distinct old-world charm, hardly ever found in your regular Mumbai police station!

BEST Electric House and Parivahan Bhavan

Situated a little ahead of the Picadilly Restaurant, on the opposite side, is the landmark BEST Electric House. Considered one of the earliest public buildings, it reflected the city's eagerness to improve the life of its citizens. Its Art Deco extension (Parivahan Bhavan) that came up much later complements the original structure. The adjacent Central Cottage Industries showroom is a big draw among foreign tourists.

In the early twentieth century, BEST (Bombay Electric Supply and Tramways Company) was responsible for supplying electricity to the city. BEST was registered in London as a subsidiary of the British Electric Traction Company, which was keen on bringing electricity to Mumbai since 1903. It secured the necessary license in 1905 and by November 1905 it started providing power to the city's tramways.

The Tramway Company that operated them was set up by Stearns and Kittredge in 1875. Its administrative offices were located near today's BEST Electric House. The company's stables were housed in Cotton Green (south-east Mumbai) and near Victoria Gardens (Veermata Jijabai Udyan) in Byculla. The first tramcars plied between Colaba and

The Colaba Police Station is celebrating its 100th year in 2006

▼

Pydhonie on 9 May 1874.

From 1930 to 1947, the supply of electricity spread across the city. Various electrical appliances were introduced to the common man. The efforts of BEST seemed to have achieved success. An important development was the setting up of a show room in 1926 on the ground floor of Electric House, to advise customers on the use of new domestic electrical appliances and about electric power in general. The service was free of charge and was aimed to promote the use of electricity. It was modelled on similar lines as in England.

The newer BEST Bhavan complex that came up much later
▼

▲
The original Electric House building

Cusrow Baug

One of the last-surviving Parsi colonies in the city, Cusrow Baug, retains the architecture and planning of a typical 'baug'. Built in the early twentieth century, a 'baug' or 'bagh' represented the extensive and well-ventilated Parsi residential complex. Apart from Cusrow Baug, the other famous Parsi colonies are Ness Baug, Jer Baug, Rustom Baug and Nowroze Baug, spread across Mumbai's tiny Parsi enclaves. Cusrow Baug was designed by the architectural firm Gregson, Batley and King as an introverted yet self-sufficient residential society with a quaint garden plan.

In 1875, the Bombay Port Trust got its first dry dock at the eastern edge of Colaba. It was built by Albert Sassoon, in memory of his father, the great Sir David Sassoon. The Sassoons were one of the earliest Baghdadi Jews to settle here

Strand Cinema

In its vicinity, old timers will remind you of the popular cinema called Strand. Now pulled down, it was a big draw among cinegoers many decades ago. One of the earliest theatres of Mumbai, it offered affordable tickets to the common man. Sadly, it was also one of the first to be affected by the glitzy cinema boom. Interestingly, the area still retains its name after all these years! This fifty-seven-year-old cinema is now all set for a revamp and should reopen by November 2006. The 15,000 square feet, 670-seater will now be sized down to a plush hall with 260 seats and will include food courts and swank interiors.

Kailas Parbat Restaurant

Situated on 1, Pasta Lane, off Shahid Bhagat Singh Marg, Kailas Parbat cannot miss the eye of the diehard foodie, in search of authentic Sindhi cuisine. Probably one of the last few restaurants to offer genuine regional cuisine in the area, it is a huge draw among the nearby resident Sindhi population who came here from across the border during Partition. Its no-frills look doesn't dissuade the hungry from stepping into this wayside restaurant.

Sassoon Docks

In 1875, the Bombay Port Trust got its first dry dock at the eastern edge of Colaba. It was built by Albert Sassoon, in memory of his father, the great Sir David Sassoon. The Sassoons were one of the earliest Baghdadi Jews to settle here. Their contribution to the city's earliest educational institutions and support for the Jewish community is well documented; Mumbai owes much to them.

The dock was excavated from solid rock with an effective depth of 18 feet

(approximately 5.5 metres). It has now ceased commission with the Mumbai Port Trust. The dock gate is another imposing structure that greets the visitor. Daily at dawn, this dock is a scene of chaotic trading as fisherfolk strike a deal for their fresh catch with interested parties; their wives prepare to sell them at fish markets all over the city and its far-flung suburbs. Baskets of shrimp, lobster, mackerel and pomfret are sold here by fisherwomen at wholesale rates, beside their colourful fishing boats bobbing on the waters of the Arabian Sea. The entire atmosphere is riotously frenzied yet intriguing.

Bombay Baptist Church and St. Xavier's Church (also called RC Church)

Walk down Shahid Bhagat Singh Marg for another ten minutes, past the Naval AIR Workshop, and you enter the MPT (Mumbai Port Trust) zone. Avoid the diversion into MPT (to your left), instead keep to the right. Walk further till you spot the Bombay Baptist Church to your left (near the junction where N. Parekh Road rejoins SBS Marg). Followers of this church inform you that the first recorded worship service for this small community was held in 1867 in Byculla, south-central Bombay. The community grew and its church was relocated in Colaba in 1911, at the present site. It was built for soldiers of the Company and residents of the area. The church was mostly served by pastors who were mainly Canadian or British. This quaint granite structure with white arches certainly deserves a look-in.

Opposite it is St. Xavier's Church famously known as RC (Roman Catholic) Church and St. Joseph's School. Another stone building with a nearly run-down outer façade manages to draw in the faithful from the vicinity. Its immediate neighbour is the Colaba Post Office. Sleepy and almost deserted, the building is hidden under shrubbery and vines.

Colaba Defence Station

This was a site tucked away on the erstwhile Colaba island chosen by the East India Company to build a cantonment for its soldiers. This decision was taken by the then Government of Bombay in 1796. Thereafter, construction of permanent houses was disallowed and it grew to become an important centre for troop activity for centuries. Commoners were prohibited from entering

The Afghan Church ▶

The entry point ▶
into the Mumbai
Port Trust zone

this high-security zone. As you enter this zone, the sea plays hide and seek on your left as a clear breeze fills the atmosphere. Wide, tree-lined roads, rows of defence establishments and residential premises transport you to a different world altogether. All this while, at a distance, a spire acts as your guide. Eventually, the road widens and you see the Afghan Church and its prominent steeple.

Afghan Church (Church Of St. John The Evangelist)

Almost half a mile from the Sick Bungalows, a temporary church was erected on Colaba Point at the entrance of the Bombay harbour, adjoining the parade ground. It was meant to benefit British soldiers stationed at the cantonment. Two years after the conquest of Kabul in 1842, Bishop Carr of Bombay wrote to the English authorities of the need to erect a church in Colaba in memory of the martyrs in Afghanistan. Its construction began in 1847. The church represents a style reminiscent of the early Classical English architecture, with walls faced with coarse Kurla rubble and plenty of fine carving in Porbander stone, the first construction in the city to put local stone to such imaginative use and also set the trend for church architecture in India. It was ideal, as it required less maintenance in the hot and muggy climate. The designs were by Henry Conybeare, the then City Engineer. Sunlight filters in through many magnificent stained glass windows. Some are beautifully detailed, depicting prophets holding scrolls and texts referring to the advent of Christ. The ceiling is of plain varnished teak while the church also boasts of a spectacular wrought iron metal screen.

The imposing Afghan Church eventually replaced the temporary chapel on 7 July 1858, when Bishop Harding consecrated the church to St. John the Evangelist. Its sky-reaching tower and steeple (sixty metres, 198 feet) was completed in 1865. It is visible from a fair distance and served as a landmark for incoming ships to the harbour in the early days. Arguably one of the city's finest examples of Gothic architecture, each piece within the church is dedicated to a deceased soldier of the Afghan campaign (in places like Kandahar and Maiwand), be it the assemblage of memorial plaques or the luminous stained glass panels decorating the bays, the china mosaic panels behind the altar or the gleaming brass worked into its flooring. Behind each name, carved in stone or brass, is a tale of martyrdom.

INHS Asvini

Situated near the Afghan Church is another establishment under the Indian Navy, known as the INHS (Indian Naval Hospital Ship) Asvini. In the 1800s, the East India Company erected buildings for invalid officers to enjoy the fresh air and for sun bathing. This building, known as the Sick Bungalows, was enclosed in a spacious complex.

Today, it's the largest of the Indian Navy's seven hospitals and comprises an 825-bed multi-specialty hospital. It is named after Asvini Kumar - the twin Vedic gods of light, supposed to bring health, happiness and inspiration from heaven to earth. Established in 1756 as the King's Seaman Hospital, INHS Asvini has a glorious history. In 1788, it was re-christened Bombay Marine Hospital. In 1863, the hospital was transferred to the Royal Army and later it served during World Wars I and II as a combined services hospital.

After Independence, the Indian Army took control and renamed it the Military Hospital, Colaba. On 1 September 1951, it was transferred to the Indian Navy and commissioned as INHS Asvini. It houses the Institute of Naval Medicine and the Marine

Medical Society.

After your visit to INHS Asvini, turn back for a detour and retrace your steps until you reach the BEST Marg. The Wesley Methodist Church greets you.

DETOUR: Wesley Methodist Church

This quaint place of worship at the junction of Shahid Bhagat Singh Marg with BEST Marg is an interesting halt. Built in the 1920s as a church for the Methodist community in the area, it represents Gothic architecture with its pristine white arches and grey stone exterior. Relatively smaller in size, this church is safe from the public gaze despite being in the heart of the Colaba Causeway, which adds to its charm.

A three-arched entrance porch opens into the sparse interior. The typical stained-glass windows tower over the entrance, bringing in the light with sections of mangled lead and missing panes. What strikes the visitor is the gigantic pipe organ near the altar, with tall gleaming metal pipes and control panels. Foot pedals and two keyboards enhance the effect. Believed to be the oldest surviving instrument of its kind in the city, the plaque on its gleaming body credits the glorious craftsmanship to Peter Conacher & Co. of Huddersfield.

Buckley Court

The original structure of Buckley Court was built in the 1920s as one of the earliest

residences on Wodehouse Road (N. Parekh Road). Today, the grey stone building is restored and exhibits the old-world charm that would greatly please restorers and historians. It is a heritage structure and thankfully, the façade of this original structure is intact. The adjoining multi-storeyed building, also known by the same name, is a towering addition to the Colaba landscape. Famous Mumbai architect Hafeez Contractor designed this eighty-five metre high-rise of twenty-five floors.

Holy Name Cathedral

The seat of the Archdiocese of Mumbai, the Cathedral is one of the most striking churches of the city. It was built in 1902 and holds an important place among the Roman Catholic community in Mumbai. The church is popularly called Wodehouse Church as it stands on Wodehouse Road.

The imposing cathedral was designed by W.A. Chambers, a noted architect, and opened for community worship in January 1905. The façade of the building is surmounted by two lofty towers, flanked on either side by the residence of the Archbishop and the Fort Convent School. An Italian Jesuit

Brother, Antono Mocheini, rendered the paintings within the church at the turn of the last century. Also within the complex, are the Archbishop's House and the Cathedral House. A sea of tranquility pervades this wooded, leafy enclosure; it almost grows on the visitor as one explores the interiors of the church. Its breathtaking interiors and restoration were the handiwork of the Czech-born Karl Schara, who transformed the cathedral into one of India's most inspired public Art Deco creations.

YMCA & CBI House

Next, you spot the YMCA building that came up in the 1920s, which offered affordable accommodation to single males in the city. This grey stone building continues with the row of similar-looking buildings along Wodehouse Road. Nearby, is the nondescript Tanna House, from where the Central Bureau of Investigation functions.

Majestic Hotel Building

Completed in 1909, this landmark

A view of Majestic hotel building

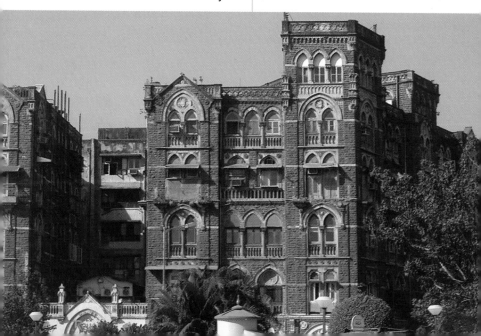

building greets one at the entrance of the Colaba Causeway on the right-hand side. It housed one of the city's earliest hotels and took the name of the building itself. Characterised by Indo-Islamic architecture, minarets and carvings on its outer façades, it stands at the junction of the Shahid Bhagat Singh Marg with the Nathalal Parekh Road and is a typical example of a corner building.

Beside the Majestic Hotel, the building houses the Shilpi Kendra, the Delhi Durbar restaurant and the Sahakari Bhandar. The Shilpi Kendra has supported Indian arts and crafts for over forty years. It hosts exhibitions throughout the year from all over India. Delhi Durbar is an old favourite, famous for its Indian and Mughlai fare and Middle Eastern ambience. Sahakari Bhandar has a co-operative department store, one of the earliest in the area for household wares; with a restaurant next door, that's popular among office-goers for its affordable Indian menu and quick service.

Mercantile Mansion

At the junction where the Nathalal Parekh Road meets Madam Cama Road are the Mercantile Mansions. Along with the Regal complex and the Majestic Buildings, it completes the famous trio of impressive yet architecturally diverse buildings as you enter the Colaba sub-precinct. This grey stone building, reduced to an almost blackish-grey exterior today, was built way back in the 1920s.

The Mercantile Mansions stand out for the solid stone exterior - reminiscent of some old rugged mansion straight out of the famous English novel *Wuthering Heights*! It has some rather interesting occupants within its corridors - Philips Antiques, Café Royal and Chunilal Mulchand & Co. Philips Antiques goes back to 1860 and is a Mecca

for antique collectors, with Victorian furniture, Portuguese collectibles and Moorish ware. One of the oldest in Colaba, Café Royal was originally an Irani café that was later renovated with plush Hollywood-styled décor. Chunilal have been makers of cinema curtains, drapes and exquisite textiles for decades.

৯০৫

Cinema, Chai and Churchgate: Mumbai's Favourite Pastimes

(Capitol Cinema - Cross Maidan - Queen's Necklace)

inema and Mumbai are integral to each other. Ask anyone from your panwallah to the white-collared executive or the south Mumbai socialite. Nobody worships cinema like the Mumbaiite. The city's love affair with films dates back to 1896 when the Lumiere Brothers' cinematograph was demonstrated to an awe-struck audience, barely six months after its inaugural showing in Paris. The Indian film industry was born in the city with the one-man film team, Dadasaheb Phalke, scripting, directing, editing and even printing *Raja Harishchandra*, India's first feature in 1912. Since then, the film industry has simply burgeoned by leaps and bounds. The Hindi film is a three-hour trip of sheer escapism so very much in sync with the Mumbaiite's psyche, that few have been left untouched by it. A huge part of this walk is devoted to some of the most popular cinemas that have enthralled city audiences for decades together.

A circuitous route, this walk also takes the curious to a few forgotten public buildings tucked away from the public glare, its earliest schools, the city's first cricket stadium, its Western Railway terminus, old hangouts as well as its most identifiable night view - the Queen's Necklace. All in all, a mixed bag with the aim of giving everyone from the bagpacker to the twenty-something a little bit of the city's intrinsic flavours and its much cherished sights and sounds.

APPROXIMATE DISTANCE
3 kilometres

APPROACH/PARKING
The best way to flag off this walk would be to reach Chhatrapati Shivaji Terminus via the suburban local train and

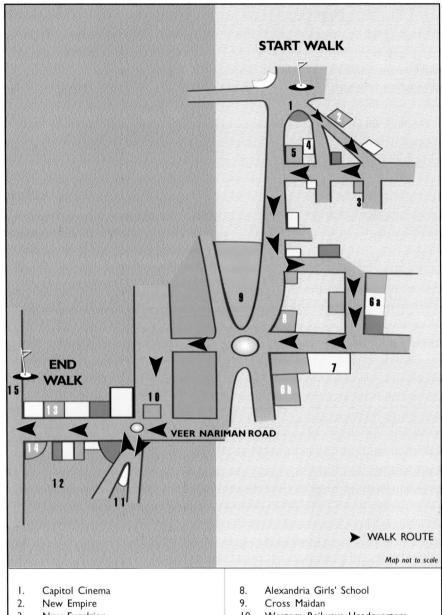

START WALK

1

2

5 4

3

9

6a

8

6b

7

END WALK

15

13

10

VEER NARIMAN ROAD

14

12

11

▶ WALK ROUTE

Map not to scale

1.	Capitol Cinema	8.	Alexandria Girls' School
2.	New Empire	9.	Cross Maidan
3.	New Excelsior	10.	Western Railways Headquarters
4.	Sterling	11.	Eros Cinema Complex
5.	Deutsche Bank	12.	Brabourne Stadium and CCI
6.	a. Cathedral & John Connon High School	13.	Hotel Ambassador
	b. Junior School	14.	Soona Mahal
7.	JB Petit School for Girls	15.	Marine Drive

hop off to reach the starting point - Capitol Cinema. It stands close to the exit of the terminus as you proceed outside from the right-hand side. Other options could be to board on any bus that is bound for Flora Fountain/Ballard Estate or Colaba and alight at the Terminus bus stop.

PLACES OF INTEREST

❖ Capitol Cinema
❖ New Empire
❖ New Excelsior
❖ Vithal's Bhelpuriwala
❖ Sterling
❖ Freemasons' Hall
❖ Deutsche Bank
❖ Educational zone - Siddharth College, Cathedral and John Connon High School, JN Petit School for Girls, Alexandria Girls' High School and Cathedral and John Connon Junior School
❖ Parsi Lying-In Hospital
❖ Atmasing Jassasing Bankebihari ENT Hospital
❖ Cross Maidan
❖ Churchgate Railway Station and the Western Railway Headquarters
❖ Eros Cinema Complex
❖ Asiatic Dept. Store
❖ Indian Merchants' Chambers
❖ Resham Bhavan
❖ Gaylord's Restaurant
❖ Brabourne Stadium & CCI
❖ Hotel Ambassador
❖ Soona Mahal Building
❖ Queen's Necklace

THE WALK

The walk begins at Capitol Cinema - one of the many theatres to have sprung up in the pre-Independence era.

Capitol Cinema

Without much of a detailed glance, one notices the jaded, lifeless exteriors of Capitol Cinema. Believe it or not, the owners of Regal Cinema also look after this dour-looking Cinema. Reduced to showing B and C-grade films, one really wonders about the stark comparison in film quality and the step-sisterly treatment meted out to Capitol. Perhaps, the cinema owners have had to yield to public pressure to sustain themselves and hence comply with the demands of screening such deplorable films to avoid being swallowed by real estate sharks.

The outer facade is typically Indo-Saracenic with white Gothic arches and granite exteriors and the structure represents an extension of several buildings along both Dr. DN Road as well as Walchand Hirachand Marg. Weeds and shrubbery can be seen sprouting out from several windows and crevices, perhaps giving the curious first-timer a clue to its ruin and eventual fate.

New Empire

Situated beside the New Empire Building (now renovated) is the New Empire Cinema. Once a hot favourite among Fort's office-goers, especially to catch a late Saturday afternoon show, this cinema seems to be going the Capitol way. At least, in terms of the steady decline of screening wholesome family entertainment.

This modern building, built along the lines of Art Deco influences, manages to draw in a motley crowd of collegians and office junta, though it's a strict no-no for those wishing to enjoy a Sunday evening show in the comfort of swish interiors, à la multiplex-style!

New Excelsior

Like its neighbours, this is one cinema that is struggling to keep up with the multiplex boom. Still frequented at times by the upmarket south Mumbaiite, its position on

▲
Capitol Cinema
Right: *New Empire Cinema*

the popularity charts has been dropping in the past decade. Poor maintenance and grubby interiors deter cinegoers from paying a visit to this cinema. Though the odd film premier does do wonders for its upkeep.

Vithal's Bhelpuriwala

En route to New Excelsior is Vithal's, the legendary bhelpuriwala of the city. Nearly half-a-century-old, it is a must-stop for first-timers, eager to taste some of the city's best loved streetside fare in the comfort of a restaurant. Vithal's may have moved to a bigger setup, yet the original flavour of their patent snack (bhel puri) remains intact.

> The cinema was a regular for children's morning shows back in the 1970s, screening films like *Alice In Wonderland* and *Tarzan*. It was also one of the first cinema halls to pay close attention towards sprucing up its lobby with attractive window displays alongside thematic stalls

Sterling

Perhaps the best-maintained of the theatres along this walk, Sterling more or less manages to retain its faithful bunch of cinegoers irrespective of the multiplex boom. One of the last surviving cinemas to exclusively screen Hollywood films, Sterling remains the most preferred of the trio. The cinema was a regular for children's morning shows back in the 1970s, screening films like *Alice In Wonderland* and *Tarzan*. It was also one of the first cinema halls to pay close attention towards sprucing up its lobby with attractive window displays alongside thematic stalls.

Symmetrical and uniform designs of the ▶ *balcony can be seen on the Jiji House building located on Damodardas Sukhadvala Marg*

Freemasons' Hall

Cinegoers to the nearby Sterling and surrounding cinemas never stop to gaze at an imposing structure that stands at the intersection of Marzban Lane with Damodardas Sukhadvala Lane. This rather stoic-looking building is the Freemasons' Hall. On 4 June 1897, His Eminence Lord Sandhurst, the then Governor of Bombay, was installed as the Grand Master (head of this community). On 5 March 1898, the present Freemasons' Hall was opened and dedicated to the community. This ceremony was performed by Lord Sandhurst, as he was the Grand Master of both the English and the Scottish Constitutions. No wonder, the main temple inside Freemasons' Hall is called the Sandhurst Temple.

The structure has a beautiful marble wall plaque of Bro. KR Cama that adorns the entrance chamber of the Freemasons' Hall. In 1886, it was Bro. John Adams (renowned city architect) who designed and supervised the construction of the throne and pedestal for the Grand Master. It continues to be in use at the Freemasons' Hall. Its yellow basalt exterior remains elusive to the public eye, frequented only by members of this largely low-profile community in the city.

Deutsche Bank
(formerly Tata Palace)

In the 1990s, Deutsche Bank undertook extensive restoration work of the Tata Palace so that its impressive, ancient façade could house the computers and executives of this financial institution. What was commendable about the restoration was retaining its original look without destroying the inner and outer façades. Building material that was in good condition was in fact reused in several parts of this white-coloured structure. Ninety-year-old tiles and Burma wood was used in substantial amounts during its renovation. The end result was a spectacular public bank, that adds character to the dull landscape along Hazarimal Somani Marg (formerly Waudby Road). In fact, it almost gives Mumbaiites their own version of the White House in the heart of the city.

Educational zone

(Siddharth College - Cathedral & John Connon Junior and High School - JN Petit High School for Girls - Alexandria Girls' High School)

Towards the north-western area of the Fort precinct, using Hazarimal Somani Marg as the compass, lie a number of schools as well as a wing of the historic Siddharth College. They lie within a radius of Maharishi Dadhichi Marg, Prescott Road, Hazarimal Somani Marg and MG Road. While the Junior High School of Cathedral & John Connon lies beside the impressive Standard Chartered Building near Flora Fountain, on Mahatma Gandhi Road, its High School is on the Maharishi Dadhichi Marg

The whitewashed, grandiose exteriors of Deutsche Bank on Hazarimal Somani Marg instantly catch the eye of the passerby
▼

The Parsi Lying-In Hospital

girls in 1860, later became The Alexandra Native Girls' School in 1863. In April 1865, the school was shifted to 31, Hazarimal Somani Marg, with a strength of 1,100!

Parsi Lying-In Hospital

Within the educational zone, the Parsi Lying-In Hospital is situated just beside the Queen's Mansion Building. Built in 1927, this rather unknown hospital is an interesting stop while taking the educational zone detour in this walk. Housed on Prescott Road, at

off Somani Marg. This school was founded in 1896. Eminent cartoonist Mario Miranda's giant-sized collage of school life at Cathedral graces the entrance of its High School wing. Just opposite is another prestigious school-the JN Petit High School for Girls.

Walk down Dadhichi Marg where the road joins up with MG Road and the Alexandria Girls' School stands to your right. It completes this quartet of historic educational centres set in splendid structures reminiscent of their glorious past and contribution to the city since the turn of the twentieth century. The Alexandra Girls' English Institution was founded by Maneckjee Cursetjee for the education of Indian girls based on Western education systems. What began as a girls' school in his own house 'Villa Byculla' with half a dozen

> The Alexandra Girls' English Institution was founded by Maneckjee Cursetjee for the education of Indian girls based on Western education systems

the turning near Queen's Mansion and the second wing of Siddharth College, it may appear as another dull-grey stone building. However, on looking closer one marvels at the intricately carved stone screens that adorn the outer walls.

The building is made of locally available blackstone and was established more than a century ago as a maternity unit for the thriving Parsi community. Today, it is a gaunt reminder of those good old days. It was set up with a capacity of forty beds but now

Above: JB Petit Girls' High School
Left: Mario Miranda's delightful depiction of school life adorns the entrance of Cathedral & John Connon High School
Below: The Atmasing Jassasing Bankebihari ENT Hospital

bears a deserted look. A magnificent new wing was recently constructed; unfortunately it is very sparsely occupied and the maternity ward has hardly any patients at all, in spite of possessing state-of-the-art operation

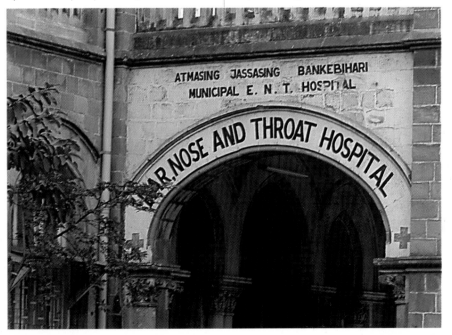

A view of some of the older heritage buildings adjoining the educational zone

theatres and other latest facilities. The old building is in dire need of repair and a fresh coat of paint, and is one of the forgotten buildings in the area.

ENT hospital

Located within the educational zone is the Atmasing Jassasing Bankebihari ENT Hospital, also known as the Municipal Hospital. Its immediate neighbours are the JB Petit School and the Cathedral & John Connon High School (junior wing). This corner building is in fact one of the oldest in these parts, dating back to the early twentieth century.

At the busy traffic signal that faces the ENT hospital, is an imposing statue of the great city father Sir Dinshaw Waccha.

Cross Maidan

Once past the signal, you see an open space that is cut in half by a pathway. This is the Cross Maidan - a grubby tuft of

land, in dire need of maintenance. Cross Maidan comprises part of the original undivided Esplanade that once stood as a wide open space overlooking the Arabian Sea at a distance. Beside it stands the Bhika Behram Well, a sacred place of worship for the Parsi community. The maidan earned its name from a stone cross that was found here, that dates back to the time when the Portuguese were in control of the city.

The Cross Maidan is the smallest of the last few open spaces in south Mumbai and is surrounded by blocks of flats on one side and trees on the other. It is rectangular in shape and evenings see a host of sports lovers, from clubside football players to cricketers who jostle for some extra space here. Another section

The Western Railway Headquarters at Churchgate was and remains a landmark of immense importance

is used to host fairs and circuses. All the same, efforts are underway to save this maidan from ruin.

Once you pass by the Cross Maidan, you spot the Ahilyabai Holkar traffic signal in front (on Veer Nariman Road). To your right stands the headquarters of the Western Railway.

Churchgate Railway Station and Western Railway Headquarters

The legacy of F.W. Stevens was carried forward with the construction of the Western Railway Headquarters. His designs were accepted in 1893 and the actual construction began in 1894 on a strip of reclaimed land on the foreshore off the Arabian Sea. The building was completed in January 1899, at a cost of Rs. 6,16,000. Blue basalt stone and white Porbander stone were used for its domes, columns and carvings. The building was replete with ornamental woodwork and wrought iron. It comprised three levels of offices and a centrally built domed tower. A prominent weathervane was perched atop this central dome. Fredrick was assisted by his son Charles and Rao Saheb Sitaram Khanderao. The headquarters represented a blend of Indo-Saracenic with a marked Venetian Gothic influence.

An integral part of the railway station culture is a bookstore chain, which is an important landmark of the Churchgate local terminus - AH Wheeler & Co., the 116-year-old living legend of the Indian Railways. This chain of bookstores has been a permanent fixture on railway platforms since 1888. But the sad news is that this chain may not get a fresh contract due to its tag of being a 'British legacy.'

Eros Cinema complex

Almost diagonally opposite the Western Railway Terminus and its suburban local terminus is the imposing Eros Cinema building. It was one of the most significant examples of the new architectonic era of Art Deco that swept across the seas from the West.

Eros was the city's second-most important Art Deco cinema, built in 1938. The entire building was designed by Bhedwar & Sorabji, who were the city's most accomplished architects of the time. The construction was dotted with interesting features - painted horizontal decorative bands, window sills and sun screens. This building was owned by Shiavax Cambata, who was eager to make Eros a replica of cinema halls

---

CULINARY MUSINGS

Walk past Churchgate Railway station every morning and you invariably see a batch of **dabbawallahs** hurriedly transferring dabbas from one handcart to another. One of the best examples of Mumbai's creative organisational ability is its unique dabba system. This is a specially tailored system of transporting dabbas (lunch containers) of home-cooked food to offices in a city where tens of thousands leave their homes at the crack of dawn to reach their workplaces across central and south Mumbai. The dabbawallahs pick up thousands of dabbas from distances up to sixty kilometers from the centre of the city, each marked with a painted hieroglyphic symbol that unlocks the mystery of its destination right down to the correct floor of the building where its hungry owner awaits it! Using a relay system, a team of runners and handcarts, the dabbas are loaded into a 'dabba special', a train exclusively meant for them, sorted out at the respective stations, from where other teams of dabbawallahs take over to deliver them, never making a mistake of delivering it to the wrong owner or being late.

---

he saw in London. The theatre boasted of a restaurant, shops and offices and even a ballroom for 500 people, complete with a spring-cushioned dance floor! This four-storeyed building's presence was further enhanced by a stepped octagonal tower. One of its most famous occupants is the Sundance

►

The Eros Cinema building complex is one the finest examples of Art Deco architecture in the city

Café - a favourite among the city's thirty-something and above crowd.

Asiatic Department Store

Long before the mall revolution invaded Mumbai, the city's populace was quite content shopping at the counters of the Asiatic Department Store on Veer Nariman Road opposite the Churchgate Railway Terminus. This department store was transformed to its present-day look from an Irani café. Unable to cope with the demands of real estate and changing choices, the café re-emerged as one of the city's most trusted department stores to date.

Indian Merchants' Chambers

The Indian Merchants' Chamber was established on 7 September 1907 in order to provide economic swaraj (independence) to India, led by stalwarts like Lokmanya Tilak, Justice Ranade, Dadabhoy Naoroji and Mahatma Gandhi. The Indian business community at the time worked towards liberating Indian industry, trade and commerce from foreign domination. It wholly supported India's political struggle and became the backbone of Indian industry. The chamber aimed at helping the economy come to terms with several setbacks in the form of wars and British oppression.

Post-Independence, the IMC was closely associated with eminent personalities like Pandit Jawaharlal Nehru, Sardar Vallabhbhai Patel, Dr Rajendra Prasad, Dr S. Radhakrishnan and Lal Bahadur Shastri. Often, the Chamber was graced by their presence and thought-provoking addresses.

The Ladies' Wing of the IMC was established in 1967 as a movement to empower women entrepreneurs who played a key role in shaping the Indian economy and industry. Today, its membership exceeds 1,400!

Resham Bhavan

Beside the IMC building is Resham Bhavan. The Synthetic & Rayon Textiles Export Promotion Council is situated in Resham Bhavan. Also located here is the FE Dinshaw Commercial & Financial Reference Library, established in 1967, as part of the Diamond Jubilee celebrations of the IMC. The aim of the library was to honour the memory of F.E. Dinshaw, a leading industrialist who played a big role in the development of steel and cement industries in India. The FE Dinshaw Memorial Trust finances the library. It provides source materials on economic, commercial and other developments in India and abroad. The Tea Board is also a resident of the Resham Bhavan. Aptly so, sitting pretty on the ground level of Resham Bhavan is the Tea Centre. This stop serves India's finest Darjeeling, Assam and Nilgiris teas along with some of the best food in the city. Breakfasts are a delight here with stuffed omlettes, waffles and cereal; lunch ranges from Oriental to traditional Parsi fare plus a most sumptuous spread of desserts

►

The Ambassador Hotel, with its revolving restaurant, is easily one of the city's most identifiable buildings along the Marine Drive skyline

Purohit, situated on Veer Nariman Road, is one of Mumbai's oldest Gujarati and first vegetarian restaurants. It was opened in 1928 at Bori Bunder and later shifted to its present address in Churchgate in 1939 opposite Brabourne stadium. In the old days, it was a favourite meeting spot for cricket fans after matches. Today, it is usually frequented by the office crowd, especially at lunch time.

from muffins and brownies to cheese cakes and apple pies.

Gaylord's Restaurant

Much before Mumbai was invaded by the café culture, a little-known bakery situated in Mayfair building on Veer Nariman Road was already a favourite among Eros cinegoers, and the bridge-playing crowd from the elite Cricket Club of India, since 1956. Gaylord's may have lost out in the race among its more youthful competitors, yet its charm remains. A warm smile greets you, the self-service operation gives the customer options galore, or if you prefer to sit back in its garden coffee shop and watch the chaotic city pass by, then its white-coloured colonial furniture is the perfect place to unwind for a restful and charming evening. And don't forget to drool and maybe, gorge on those chocolate truffle pastries while you're there!

Brabourne Stadium and Cricket Club of India

The Governor of the city in the 1930s Lord Brabourne, was a great follower of cricket. The Brabourne Stadium at the Cricket Club of India was named after him. The stadium was built on a piece of reclaimed land which Governor Brabourne handed over to the Cricket Club of India. The architects Gregson, Batley and King drew up the designs for this historic cricket stadium. The inaugural match was held here in 1937 between the CCI and Lord Tennyson's XI after it was officially opened on 7 December 1937. The stadium boasted a seating capacity of 40,000 and came equipped with a state-of-the-art clubhouse, billiards room, tennis and badminton courts and swimming pool. Almost every historic tournament in cricket, Ranji (inter-state) as well as international matches were played here until the nearby Wankhede Stadium was completed in 1974. Since then, the huge stadium is used for other national and international sports meets and occasionally for recreational activities.

The headquarters of the Board of Control for Cricket in India (BCCI) was previously housed within the stadium's premises before it was shifted to its present office at Eden Gardens, Kolkata in the early 1990s.

Along this stretch, one sees some of the oldest establishments like K. Rustom & Sons - the old favourite bakery among Churchgate's residents (don't miss having your new ice cream box filled here!) and Wordell Chemists, established in 1954 as well as the now closed Cruzon Studio (one wonders why its signboard is still very much on display!).

In fact, this entire stretch towards Marine Drive on both sides of Veer

Marine Drive remains the most prominent and ► popular sea-facing promenade of the city, its fast-moving traffic representative of the city's frenetic pace

Nariman Road, is lined with restaurants, cafes and bakeries that serve you some of the city's finest foods. To sum it up, Tea Centre for sandwiches, Shiv Sagar for its Udupi fare, Not Just Jazz By The Bay for the music, seaside view and food, Kamling for the authentic Chinese experience - the list is endless.

Hotel Ambassador

The most famous restaurant at the Hotel Ambassador is easily the Oriental dining bar - Pearl Of The Orient, started in .981 as Mumbai's first revolving restaurant. A huge draw, it still remains a one of a kind in the city. This beautifully designed eatery serves some of the finest Oriental food - Korean, Thai, Chinese and Japanese - even as it offers a breathtaking view of Mumbai. While atop, it provides the onlooker with a spectacular canvas of the city's vibrancy, especially at night. The hotel chain is also behind the popular fast food restaurants - 'Croissants Etc.'

Next door is the Chateau Windsor Hotel, another Art Deco building along Veer Nariman Road. This building has all the trappings of the old world, from its spacious entrance, wooden interiors, not forgetting its elevator that looks like it could be on Bond Street, London!

Soona Mahal

Built in the 1930s, this building overlooking the Arabian Sea remains one of the most visible examples of the Art Deco skyline that gradually took over the Mumbai building architecture from the 1930s and 1940s. These buildings were characterised by constructions using stipulated height control, hence the similarity.

A typical feature of such buildings were rounded balconies, corner pavilions of terraces and Art Deco motifs embossed and painted on these buildings. Soona Mahal's most famous occupant was Jazz By The Bay, the hotbed for the city's jazz fraternity who assembled here for impromptu performances and jam sessions. The nucleus of the current crop of jazz performers was formed and nurtured at this very sacred Mecca. In the early 1990s, there was only Jazz By The Bay. For over two and a half years, it exclusively catered to the jazz-loving audience of Mumbai by featuring live jazz performances every night. Jazz lovers lapped it up. Unfortunately, the number of jazz fanatics in Mumbai dwindled and as the clientele got younger and the younger clientele got richer, there was a demand for more variety in the music. A couple of years later, the prefix 'Not Just' was added to the name and thus was born Not Just Jazz By The Bay. Live performances take place seven days a week. Music ranges from rock, blues, fusion and yes, jazz. Some of the better bands of Mumbai play here. Today, it has transformed itself into its swanky new version and may no longer remain an all-jazz haven, but it continues to draw in some of the city's most serious music lovers. With its subtle interiors, great menu and live music shows everyday, it attracts a more sophisticated clientele.

Marine Drive - Queen's Necklace

Prior to the 1920s, this was a stretch of restless azure sea, but when this strip of land was reclaimed along the Backbay, it transformed itself into one of the most recognisable parts of this city and easily one of the most beautiful promenades. The entire drive was more or less complete by 1940. Marine Drive stretches from Nariman Point and sweeps around Chowpatty Beach before it ends at Malabar Hill. The curve, rimmed by neon lights produces a most spectacular view at night, like a string of pearls drawn across this dramatic curve. No wonder it is referred to as the 'Queen's Necklace.' Most of Marine Drive runs along Queen's Road, now renamed Netaji Subhash Chandra Bose Road. This stretch, with its parapet and broad pavement that runs throughout, is a favourite haunt for breeze-lovers, joggers and walkers who throng it at any given time of the day. It is also the ideal place to enjoy some roasted buttery bhutta (corn), especially in the monsoon, and groundnuts throughout the year. Horse-drawn Victoria rides are available from either end of the promenade. A number of residential buildings, mostly built in the Art Deco style with a uniform height and design, are lined up along the opposite side of the road complementing this magnificent promenade.

ॐ

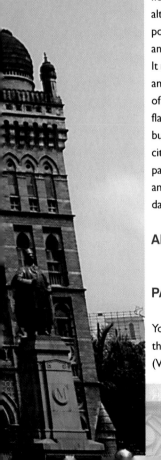

The Great Indian Diaspora: Kalbadevi, Princess Street and Dhobi Talao

(BMC Building - Dhobi Talao - Princess Street - Liberty Cinema)

f you thought Mumbai's heritage was all about Gothic structures, sprawling Victorian mansions, libraries and towering church spires, well-laid out circles and causeways, this walk promises some delightful surprises. It takes you through the arterial heartland of the old city. Here, traditional businesses flourished and life assumed a slower pace. A different world altogether, it kept a safe distance from the British town and all its pomp and splendour. Life was simple; trading was the mainstay and communities from all over the country made it their home. It represented an ideal example of different communities working and living together in a locality that spread across the outer limits of the Fort. Till today, several parts of this region retain their old flavour. Buildings are in dire need of repair and conventional business thrive, yet remain hidden from the glare of the bustling city outside. A frail octogenarian Parsi will meet you as you walk past the agiary, tempt you with some bun-maska at the nearby café and take you back in time to the good old days…you listen. Such days are rare and precious.

APPROXIMATE DISTANCE
3 kilometres

PARKING/APPROACH
Reaching the starting point of this walk shouldn't be a bother. You will immediately spot the Municipal Corporation building the moment you get off a local train at the Chhatrapati Shivaji (Victoria) Terminus. If you have a private vehicle then parking

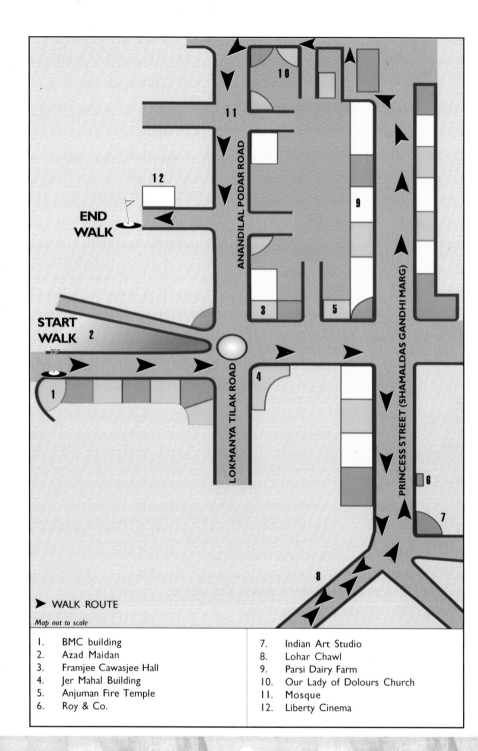

END WALK

START WALK

ANANDILAL PODAR ROAD

LOKMANYA TILAK ROAD

PRINCESS STREET (SHAMALDAS GANDHI MARG)

► WALK ROUTE

Map not to scale

1.	BMC building	7.	Indian Art Studio
2.	Azad Maidan	8.	Lohar Chawl
3.	Framjee Cawasjee Hall	9.	Parsi Dairy Farm
4.	Jer Mahal Building	10.	Our Lady of Dolours Church
5.	Anjuman Fire Temple	11.	Mosque
6.	Roy & Co.	12.	Liberty Cinema

along the pavement of Mahapalika Marg is an arduous proposition. Especially since you may need to hustle for space with long-faced lawyers and grim-looking administrators.

PLACES OF INTEREST

- ❖ Greater Mumbai Municipal Corporation Building
- ❖ Azad Maidan
- ❖ Metropolitan Magistrate's Court
- ❖ Cama and Albless Hospital
- ❖ St. Xavier's College
- ❖ State Technical Education Department
- ❖ Framjee Cawasjee Institute
- ❖ Jer Mahal Building
- ❖ Kyani and Bastani cafés (now closed)
- ❖ BX Furtado & Sons and LM Furtado & Sons
- ❖ David & Co.
- ❖ Anjuman Fire Temple
- ❖ Dhobi Talao Market
- ❖ Princess Street - Lohar Chawl - Parsi Dairy Farm and adjoining buildings
- ❖ Our Lady of Dolours Church on Maharshi Karve Road
- ❖ 1st Marine Street (Anandilal Podar Road)
- ❖ Liberty Cinema

THE WALK

This walk leads you into the heart of the city's civic and administrative nucleus - the trading hinterland that mushroomed since the late eighteenth century. Precarious-looking buildings, narrow bylanes and old-fashioned businesses don't paint a pretty picture, yet they remain clothed in history with their own tales to tell. You can sense the city's famed business acumen and eagerness to succeed as you walk through these parts. Let's begin at the imposing BMC Building, the guiding light that keeps our city alive and in good shape.

BMC Building (Greater Mumbai Municipal Corporation, also called the Corporation Building)

This public building facing the Terminus complements it and together, they represent one of the most recognisable landscapes of the city. The magnificent domed and miniature structure is a spectacular blend of Gothic and Oriental architecture, designed by F.W. Stevens and opened in 1893. The tower measures seventy-eight metres (255 feet) and is capped by a splendid dome. Octagonal-shaped minarets flank its corners and the building has Gothic-styled arched double windows. In fact, RF Chisholm's first-prize-winning Indo-Saracenic design for this building was the initial choice. But the administration at that time favoured the Gothic style as the official 'Bombay style' and so his plans were bypassed and F.W. Stevens' design was chosen. The Corporation Hall inside is closely based on Birmingham's Council Chamber and the Glasgow Municipal Building.

Over the central gable, on its south side is a four metre high (thirteen feet) allegorical statue representing the title that was conferred upon and adopted by the city - 'Urbs Primus In Indis' - with the arms of the Municipal Corporation contained in a circular panel beneath it. At the entrance of the building is a statue of Sir Pherozeshah Mehta, who played an invaluable role in the city's early civic administration and was responsible for the drafting of its earliest laws. Others who played a key role in the establishment of the city's municipal corporation were Sir Dinshaw Wacha, Manmohandas Ramji and Purshottamdas Thakoredas.

Azad Maidan

Part of the formerly undivided Esplanade, Azad Maidan constitutes a section of the northern end of this huge open space that once stretched from Cooperage to Lohar Chawl. This maidan is parallel to the Mahapalika Marg and plays host to rallies, morchas and public gatherings throughout the year. Besides, it is home to countless cricket pitches where scores of wannabe Tendulkars hone their skills to don the Indian cricket team colours. A section of the Azad Maidan is also home to the Mumbai School Sports Association, an organisation that strives for the betterment of all sport at the school level.

Azad Maidan
▼

Metropolitan Magistrate's Court

Adjacent to the BMC Building, is another public structure related to the lawmaking in the city - the Chief Metropolitan Magistrate's Court. This building, a hotbed of legal activity throughout the year, also sports the typically faded yellow basalt and granite exterior.

Cama and Albless Hospital

Next in the line of view is the Cama and Albless Hospital, only meant for women and children. The hospital is enclosed in a sprawling campus amidst verdant and wooded surroundings. The original hospital is an old construction along the Mahapalika Marg and the new wing was added later to accommodate the increasing needs of the city's population. This hospital came up after Mahapalika Road (Cruickshank Road) was laid out in the early twentieth century and was one of the earliest to cater to the needs of women and children of the city. The Federation of Obstetric & Gynaecological Societies of India is housed here. In fact, with its dull exterior the Hospital can easily pass off as just another sleepy government establishment.

St. Xavier's College

▼

St. Xavier's College

One of the leading and earliest educational establishments in the city, St. Xavier's College was founded by Jesuit priests in 1867. Father Wagner designed its main building. It exhibits a fine tower surmounted by a statue of the patron saint, St. Francis Xavier.

The college was named after St. Francis Xavier, the scholar and patron saint of the Jesuit community. On 30 January 1869, St. Xavier's was affiliated to the University of Bombay. The college was in the forefront of equal education, and women were first granted admission in 1912. Between 1900-10, it experienced a period of further expansion

The Framjee Cawasjee Hall and Reading Room at Dhobi Talao

and the building plan for a new structure on Cruickshank Road was ready.

In 1925, renowned research scholar Fr. H. Heras began work on the Indian Historical Research Institute. Being the college librarian, he could undertake ceaseless research work and supported students in their research. With time, students pursued their Masters and Ph.D. degrees and this institute, backed by the wholehearted support of Fr. Heras, took shape. As a sign of respect and to honour the work of Fr. Heras, the institute was renamed after him, after his death in 1955. Today, this institute is home to an exhaustive collection of historical books, documents, pamphlets and countless printed writings. The Institute attracts several researchers, scholars, and writers from all parts of the globe.

State Technical Education Department

Next in this line of public buildings is the State Department of Technology followed by the Elphinstone Technical School campus. Both buildings have a uniform appearance from the outside. Dull, granite and with faded yellow basalt exteriors, leafy surroundings and a general air of tranquility pervade these surroundings, compared to the hustle and bustle outside.

Once you reach the chaotic Dhobi Talao traffic junction, all of a sudden, the surroundings undergo a change. Crammed buildings with little or no breathing space between them and narrower roads greet you. After you pass the St. Xavier's School to your right, the Framjee Cawasjee Institute and Reading Hall can be seen opposite the Jer Mahal building.

Framjee Cawasjee Institute and Hall

The Framjee Cawasjee Institute and Reading Hall is located at the Dhobi Talao Junction along 1st Marine Street. A statue of a learned Parsi Kavasji Petigara stands near its

◄ *A closer view of Jer Mahal building
at the entrance into Dhobi Talao*

western exit, erected way back in 1940 with public subscription. Its main entrance faces the Metro Cinema building. The building stands out for its brightly-coated exteriors, in stark contrast to the surrounding structures, most of which seem to have faded with time and sheer neglect.

Beside Cawasjee Hall stands the People's Free Reading Room and Library housed in the N.Wadia General Library. This structure faces the Jer Mahal building and lies at the beginning of Sir Jagannath Shankarseth Road (formerly Girgaum Road).

Jer Mahal

Overlooking the Dhobi Talao intersection, where the Lokmanya Tilak Road meets with the Jagannath Shankarseth Road, stands the ominous yet run-down commercial and residential building - Jer Mahal. This semi-circular building is the typical corner structure,

with businesses like the famous music salons from Furtado & Sons (BX Furtado and LM Furtado), Great Punjab Hotel, Bombay Sports, Kashmir Hotel, Wellington Hairdressers, Richie Rich Trophies and Awards, Jhaveri Bros and Kyani Bakery.

Its period-styled wooden balconies collapsed some time ago. Restoration work began and was stalled due to lack of funds. The original artwork and carvings of its unique balconies are extremely crucial to the exterior of this landmark in Dhobi Talao.

The Irani Café (Kyani and Bastani)

The Kyani and Bastani cafés together represent the very soul of the Irani café's existence in the city. While Bastani had to shut down last year, falling prey to spurious commercialisation, Kyani still holds its own. Wooden chairs, red-checkered tablecloths, the picture of Zarathustra, huge glass jars holding bakery-made Shrewsbury and wine biscuits or freshly-made mava cakes, wooden pillars with mirrors, glass-cased shelves displaying the day's baked goodies, portraits of the Shah of Iran and a blackboard with a long list of dos and don'ts - that's your typical Irani cafe! Kyani & Co. actually celebrated its 100th birthday in 2004.

Bastani's was famous for its chicken biryani and kheema-pau. Both cafes were favourite haunts for students of St. Xavier's College. The other popular cafes included the Sassanian Boulangerie at Dhobi Talao for its Parsi food and New Excelsior café (now closed down) also for its kheema-pau. What was common with all these cafés was their watery, milky tea, and the laid-back atmosphere.

So integral is the Irani café to Mumbai's culture that both cinema and theatre have incorporated this segment of our society. In fact, writer-director Shiv Subramanyam, best

known for his screenplays of Vidhu Vinod Chopra's *Parinda* and *1942: A Love Story*, staged his play *Irani Cafe* at the Prithvi Theatre Festival in 2002.

BX Furtado & Sons and LM Furtado & Co.

Almost as old as their Irani neighbours is the legacy of the famous Furtado & Sons. Set up by two Goan brothers back in 1886, the firm 'BX (Bernardo Xavier) Furtado' was even listed in *The Times Of India* Calendar and Directory. Apparently, at some point its venue was changed. For some years, his younger brother, Luis Manoel, collaborated till he established himself as an independent firm, in the neighbourhood in a friendly rivalry. In 1914, the firm BX Furtado & Sons moved to its present site within the newly constructed Jer Mahal Building at Dhobi Talao where, although under a different management, it remains an important landmark in the city.

◄ *Such boards are a regular sight in most Irani cafes*

Today, they continue to make the city dance to their tunes. Well, almost! Both establishments stock an enviable range of musical instruments from Yamaha keyboards to cool red drum sets that remind you of some 1950s Hollywood Elvis-starrer. It is a place most sought after by a guitar-crazy collegian as well as a septuagenarian jazz aficionado. The lack of any flashy neon signposts or shiny exteriors may flatter to deceive but step into either of these two stores and chances of walking out without your preferred buy are rare. The owners will take you back in time, with quirky anecdotes about its indelible contribution to the city's musicians and famous bands. The warmth and personal attention is a rarity these days. Perhaps, representative of this part of the city -untouched by the outside world.

With the lifting of restrictions on the import of musical instruments in 1994, the Furtados have quite a few firsts to their credit, like:

- The first to import acoustic pianos.
- The first to import electric and acoustic guitars, wind and brass instruments.
- The first to import music composing and sequencing software.

A walk down Shankarseth Road and you spot several old buildings on either side. The first of these to your left is the Palkhivala Building, home to an old resident that dates back to more than fifty years - Brabourne Restaurant, second-hand bookstores and record companies. You come across quaint-sounding bylanes like Jambul Vadi (this lane must have been lined by jambul (berry) trees at some point in time) and Navjeevan Vadi and even building names seem to narrate their own tales - Bhiwandiwala Mansion (maybe the builder

These Parsis settled in the central localities around the Talao and often acted as middlemen for the British as they understood English and were highly preferred over the other Indian communities to do business with the Company

hailed from nearby Bhiwandi in Thane district!) and Sharaf Manzil with its low-key occupant, a big hit among the city's Christian population for very interesting reasons...welcome to David & Co.!

David & Co.

At the very mention of wedding invites, to a Christian family planning a wedding, pat comes the response - David & Co. Dating back to 1936, this store is a huge draw among the community. Other huge orders for invites are usually for First Holy Communions and wedding anniversaries. Customers flock here to get their orders done well in advance, before the wedding season begins. Though virtually hidden from public gaze, it's almost unbelievable to imagine how integral David & Co. is to the average Christian family!

Of course, everyone including the

▲

The Anjuman Fire Temple on
Sir J. Shankarseth Road

owner will admit how things have changed over the years, with trendier, more fashionable invites made of expensive, 'handmade' paper preferred over the good old white 'n silver-coloured wedding invite. But then, they have survived and are a name to reckon with even in this day and age.

Anjuman Fire Temple

Beside the Bhiwandiwala Mansion is the Anjuman fire temple, established way back in 1783 to cater to the Parsi population who lived along Princess Street and the nearby Dhobi Talao region. This agiary is relatively smaller than its more prominent neighbour a few blocks ahead - the Wadia Atash Behram.

An air of solemnity pervades throughout despite being in the heart of a crowded hinterland.

Most Parsis made this area their home, when the city's Fort area began to get congested with its rapidly burgeoning population. The affluent families decided to move out of the crowded confines inside the Fort and settled along these outer limits of the city, which is the Dhobi Talao region of today. These Parsis settled in the central localities around the Talao and often acted as middlemen for the British as they understood English and were highly preferred over the other Indian communities to do business with the Company.

Dhobi Talao Market

As you brace yourself to enter this bustling

area you spot another remnant of the old days, Alfred Restaurant situated in Chandan Mahal, also on J. Shankarseth Road.

You proceed ahead into the highly congested inner lanes of the old city; this area is sometimes also referred to as Kalbadevi, though the area extends way beyond the route of this walk. According to historians, in the early 1800s, the Back Bay foreshore was lined with the Esplanade barracks, known as Marine Lines. A tiny settlement of service people grew around it, and a nearby tank where soldiers' uniforms were laundered went on to adopt the name of 'Washerman's Tank' or Dhobi Talao.

The Dhobi Talao market will unnerve you with its mayhem, congested lanes, frenetic pace and above all, a sea of humanity. This densely populated area is one of the busiest areas of trading activity. Establishments range from pharmaceuticals and rose-scented perfumes to garish-looking chandeliers straight out of a 1960s Bollywood family melodrama in Technicolour!

The walk covers two integral parts of this maze of interconnected lanes - Lohar Chawl and Princess Street.

Princess Street

Step into Princess Street (Shamaldas Gandhi Marg) and take a right turn near Cooper Building. This part of Princess Street could well be renamed 'Pharma Street' for the rows of pharmaceutical establishments that jostle for space along this stretch. There are stores selling homemade remedies - homeopath and allopathic medicines, traditional medications, optical and surgical equipment. Medical equipment meant for homebound patients is available on hire. Some of the oldest surviving pharmacies include Roy & Co. Homoeopaths (established in 1889) along with countless Parsi homeopathic pharmacies. Once again, the first-timer will notice how this part is hardly touched by commercialisation. Wooden counters, old-style markings on medicine shelves, rickety ladders, dull signboards and chemist attendants the age of your grandfather greet you with a warm smile. Time stands still here.

◄ *Roy & Co.—one of the city's oldest surviving pharmacists—on Princess Street*

Local perfumes are sold in many outlets, and seem to be a flourishing business. Maybe not for the upmarket Davidoff and Dior fans, but they do spurn your senses with terribly strong fragrances!

Along this stretch, most of the landscape is mundane and doesn't exactly enthrall the visitor. The chaos, coupled with a general business-like air may not make for a quiet walk down memory lane. You have to crane your neck to spot the odd historic building or stumble upon some architecturally brilliant construction. Yet the hidden-world feel grows on you. One landmark that grabs your attention is the Indian Art Studio within the Gold Mohur Building. Situated in a typical corner building, complete with arched windows, reminiscent of the splendid Gothic buildings in the Fort area, this studio is well known for photo restorations and canvas paintings. You can almost sense the flashbulbs of yore as you enter this studio. Smiling black and white photographs of some grand Parsi baronet with his family stare back at you, even the late actress Madhubala can be spotted with her luminous smile, as the owner proudly displays his acquisitions. Some older cameras, film rolls and albums are also on display in this little treasure trove from the past.

From the Indian Art Studio, the road splits in two directions. Take the road to the right-hand side to enter Lohar Chawl. The area earned its name after the earliest shops of ironmongers that were set up here in the late 1800s. This part of Princess Street is home to scores of establishments that house practically everything needed to light up

◄

The corner building Gold Mohur, on Princess Street, houses the famous Indian Art Studio

your world. Scarlet-hued bulbs, fancy lamps, snake-like electric tubes, chandeliers fit for Arab sheikhs, ghastly lampshades, slender wiring - it remains the final stop for electrical equipment and accessories. Wholesalers, retailers, small-time shopkeepers have all been bound to this place for decades together.

Take a U-turn after the 'Light show' at Lohar Chawl and walk back to the intersection of Princess Street and J. Shankarseth Road. Right there, at the crossing on the ground floor of Cooper Building is the Parsi establishment called Faredoon & Burjor. This corner shop is a must stop for the Parsi faithful. It caters to every need of the Parsi - sudras, vests, particulars meant for rituals and prayers.

Across the road, towards the other side of Princess Street, the Parsi flavour is still obvious. Sopariwala Building, Guzder Mansion, Sidhwa Building (1915) and the street's most popular occupant - The Parsi Dairy Farm. Established in 1895, it remains

The Parsi Dairy Farm on Princess Street is one of the most famous landmarks in Dhobi Talao

famous for its wholesome milk and calorie-packed kulfis. This isn't a restaurant but more of a take-away shop. Its sparkling -clean interiors and high-quality Indian cream sweets such as badam burfi (made with crushed almonds) or rabri (a decadently rich desert) are to die for.

Two schools also dot this street - The Sir JJ Princess Street School and The Bai Manekbai Gumadia School for Girls. You spot old watch repair stores, chemists, hair salons, opticians, frame and furniture traders, and tiny restaurants - very much out of sync with the neon landscape that lies in its periphery.

Once you approach the end of Princess Street, near Guzdar Mansion, take a left turn as you enter the back alleys of Princess Street. A similar landscape guides you and just then,

> At the crossing on the ground floor of Cooper Building is the Parsi establishment called Faredoon & Burjor. This corner shop is a must stop for the Parsi faithful

an interesting signboard catches your attention. It reads Alcoholics Anonymous. A scurrying passerby tells you that this place attracts people from all over and remains one of the oldest in the city. All of a sudden, strains of a saxophone fill the air, the cymbals join in and drumbeats also become party to this session. It lends an almost eerie break to the silence of the alley. Quite a few marriage and funeral bands practise here, I am informed. A right turn from this crossroad will lead you to Maharshi Karve Road and soon you come face-to-face with the arches of Our Lady of Dolours Church.

Our Lady of Dolours Church

This church is located on Maharshi Karve Road, and has a large following of devotee because of its 'miraculous' cross. The cross — frequented by thousands of worshippers everyday—stands in an area of 700 sq. feet.

1st Marine Street

Leave the church and the road behind you is known as 1st Marine Street (Anandilal Podar Marg). This street is home to the famous MM Poonjiaji & Sons, pickle-makers since 1883; the ever-popular café called Sassanian Boulangerie Restaurant and Bakery; and the Thackers vegetarian restaurant. For all the vegetarians of the city, Thackers, is like a breath of fresh air. Today, it is jazzed up beyond recognition by architect Hafeez Contractor. It is famous for its tirangi dhoklas, methi theplas and sakkarkan nu undhiyu. The best of Surti Gujarati food in Class 1 comfort is on offer here.

Sassanian, housed in Marine Building, will tempt you with their lip-smacking plum cakes, hot chicken puffs and yummy caramel custards. The rates are shockingly low and the place is another example of the Irani café culture's hold over the city's populace. In the late 1800s, MM Poojiaji first started making chutneys to suit British tastes. Its instant success and popularity found Poonjiaji being appointed as his Excellency, the Governor of Bombay's official supplier. Today, even over a century, the firm continues to create a whole range of chutneys, pickles, condiments, pastes and spices to suit every palate.

An interesting mosque is the one at Dhobi Talao, right in the middle of 1st Marine Street, which serves as a traffic island. On a Friday afternoon, you will find scores of taxis parked in the street and taxi-drivers offering namaz. It is locally referred to as the 'taxi-driver's mosque.'

Liberty Cinema

You're nearing the end of this walk. What better place to cool your heels than within the plush, art-deco interiors of Liberty Cinema. Enter Vithaldas Thackersey Road, situated off Marine Street and you come face to face with another of the city's old-time cinemas - Liberty. This regal theatre opened with *Andaz*, which ran for two years from 1949-52! In fact, much later, in the 1990s, Rajshri Productions' blockbuster *Hum Aapke Hain Kaun* did 2,341 shows in 847 days of its run at this cinema. It ran for 105 weeks in regular shows and sixteen weeks in noon shows. So popular were the outfits of *Hum Apke Hain Kaun* that they were showcased in Mumbai's Liberty theatre, a few weeks after the film's release.

৪০৫

Liberty Cinema
▼

The Inner City: Mumbai's Unchanged Heart

(Girgaum - Khotachiwadi - Opera House)

Welcome to the very heart of the Indian township, untouched, unscathed and in a world of its own - Girgaum. This area began to take shape in the mid-nineteenth century and its planning is virtually intact, except for the tarred roads and pedestrian pathways. This area—all the way up to that famous and now forgotten old lady of Indian theatre, the Royal Opera House—will entice the first timer to take more than a peek into what was once the early city and its narrow, hidden bylanes. Here, one gets the feeling of living in a time several decades behind the present! Traffic may whiz past these roads, highrises may have sprouted in its less-than-flashy skyline, yet most of its populace, along with their businesses, have remained relatively unchanged since the early 1900s...which augurs well for the city, desperate to hold on to its past. Its crowded bazaars, its people, its temples, churches, the wadis, the chawls - all of them have their own stories to tell. So, without further delay let's step into this charming little world, never mind the feeling of claustrophobia that might just engulf the first-timer!

APPROXIMATE DISTANCE
3.5 kilometres

PLACES OF INTEREST
- ❖ Wadiaji Atash Behram
- ❖ Chira Bazaar
- ❖ Bylanes off J. Shankarseth Road - Gaiwadi, Kandewadi, Mangalwadi
- ❖ Goan Institute Building and St. Francis Xavier Church
- ❖ Majestic Cinema

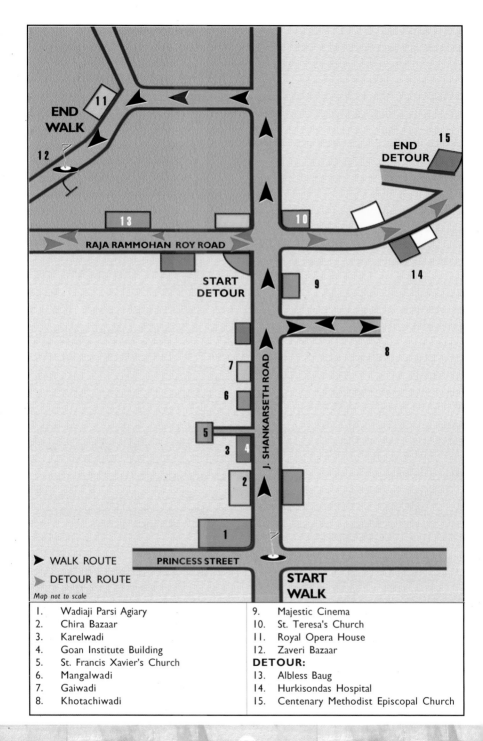

END WALK

11

12

13

RAJA RAMMOHAN ROY ROAD

START DETOUR

7

6

5

3 4

2

1

J. SHANKARSETH ROAD

PRINCESS STREET

10

END DETOUR

15

14

9

8

START WALK

▶ WALK ROUTE
▶ DETOUR ROUTE
Map not to scale

1.	Wadiaji Parsi Agiary	9.	Majestic Cinema
2.	Chira Bazaar	10.	St. Teresa's Church
3.	Karelwadi	11.	Royal Opera House
4.	Goan Institute Building	12.	Zaveri Bazaar
5.	St. Francis Xavier's Church	**DETOUR:**	
6.	Mangalwadi	13.	Albless Baug
7.	Gaiwadi	14.	Hurkisondas Hospital
8.	Khotachiwadi	15.	Centenary Methodist Episcopal Church

- ❖ Khotachiwadi
- ❖ St. Teresa's Church
- ❖ **DETOUR:** Albless Baug - Central Plaza Cinema - Prarthana Samaj - Hurkisondas Hospital - Parsi Agiary on R. Roy Road - Magistrate's Building - Centenary Methodist Episcopal Church
- ❖ Royal Opera House
- ❖ Zaveri Bazaar - Tribhovandas Bhimji Zaveri

THE WALK

This walk takes you to the heart of Mumbai's industrious and traditional business districts. Quite literally. From the assembly-line images of nondescript shops, jostling for space along Girgaum's roads and markets to the boisterous crowds at Zaveri Bazaar, this stretch winds its way through Mumbai's bustling, crowded arterial roads. Nothing impressive about it, one may think. But walk along these roads and you will savour and experience the essence of the traditional Indian street, its residences and the general buzz of the original Indian bazaar.

Wadiaji Atash Behram

This fire temple situated at the junction of Princess Street and Sir Jagannath Shankarseth Road is one of the oldest in the city. Built in 1830, it is patronised by the Parsi population who built their homes and businesses here, way back in early 1800, just after the Great Fire in the Fort, in 1803. At the time, thousands of Parsi families had to seek refuge in Dhobi Talao and Girgaum.

This area was formerly called Charni Wadi, from the grazing ground for cattle that once stood here. Later, the area was collectively called 'Chandanwadi' for the many sandalwood stores that came up nearby and remain to this day. The present fire temple was built by the three sons of Hormusji Wadia. Twenty-five years before, Hormusji built a fire temple in the same compound where this fire temple stands. A part of the Atash Behram fire is from a sacred

Parsi agiary situated at the junction of Princess Street and Sir J. Shankarseth Road

▼

◀ *Rows of jewellery shops dot the Sir J. Shankarseth Road. These include the local favourite Waman Hari Pethe Jewellers, established way back in 1908*

The two busts of bulls that adorn ▶ the entrance into Gaiwadi, Sir J. Shankarseth Road

fire that was brought all the way from Calcutta (now Kolkata). In October 1929, this sacred fire was used in the making of the Wadia Atash Behram fire.

This building, evasive to the public eye, is only open to followers of the Zoroastrian faith. Built in typical Indo-Iranian architectural style, one can spot fluted columns, verandahs and even bull capitals that adorn this Porbander stone structure.

Chira Bazaar

At the start of this stretch that can be referred to as Girgaum, is Chira Bazaar (locally referred to as the 'gold market'). It lies along Shankarseth Road and remains the nucleus of the jewellery market in middle-class Girgaum. This market is a huge draw among both the Maharashtrian and Christian communities. Most shops here date back to the 1940s and '50s and have stuck to their traditional ways of retail. While the designs are unmistakably local, keeping in mind the resident population, one cannot but marvel at the manner in which these shops have remained virtually untouched by the presence of glitzy showrooms and commercial establishments that are less than a stone's

DID YOU KNOW?

Girgaum Road was renamed Sir Jagannath Shankarseth Road (spelling varies along different parts of this area) after a prominent nineteenth century resident of Girgaum. He was known as a visionary and leader who took up various causes of people in those times and was respected for his contribution to society. Further down, towards central Mumbai, the Dadar T.T. Circle flyover is renamed after him.

throw away. Waman Hari Pethe Jewellers, (established in 1908) one of the oldest jewellers is a landmark here. The entire stretch, also known as Kamani Wadi, is dotted with nondescript-looking jewellery shops.

Girgaum Road (now Sir Jagannath Shankarseth Road) and its bylanes

Girgaum, at the foot of Malabar Hill, takes its name from the Sanskrit words giri

(mountain) and grama (village). Enter this heartland of the city's Marathi-speaking population and its middle-class environs, the area provides for a fascinating insight into Mumbai's oldest parts, and how they have remained largely untouched and unscathed by commercialisation. It is replete with 'urban villages' - narrow streets sprinkled with temples, fire temples, churches and quaint bazaars. What strikes you almost immediately

about this long, winding road, apart from its old businesses and rustic ambience are the interesting names of its bylanes. Mangalwadi, Gaiwadi, Kandewadi, Ambewadi are just some of the names that catch your attention.

Incidentally, the particular produce of the land led to the naming of the area, especially in bylanes and alleys through Shankarseth Road. A wadi is the vernacular name for a garden, orchard or a plantation, and various plantation estates in the early city were known after the produces generated by them such as Phanaswadi, Bhorbhat Lane, Mugbhat Lane, Jambulwadi, Kelawadi, Karelwadi, Ambewadi, Kandewadi and Nicadwadi, (named after various fruits, vegetables, pulses etc). Gaiwadi is an exception, probably named after cowsheds that were situated in this lane. In fact, at the entrance of Gaiwadi, look closely and spot the busts of two bulls, made in yellow granite, now aged with time and neglect.

Most wadis are distinguished by low rise and high density housing with unique

Girgaum during Ganeshotsav festivities
▼

architectural and cultural nuances. The other classification of the wadi is on the basis of religion or caste. Bhangwadi, Popatwadi, Dabholkarwadi and Khotachiwadi are some of the wadis scattered over Mumbai. Khotachiwadi is named after Dadoba Waman Khot, a land revenue officer. The progress of these wadis is quite detached and they retain much of their traditional architecture that reflects daily life patterns.

Some of the newer establishments that have sprung up are textile stores, shoe and stationery shops, besides the traditional provision stores to cater to the local populace. Most of them came up in the 1930s and '40s and have remained intact since then. You will

GOAN INSTITUTE BUILDING

▲
Goan Institute Building on
Sir J. Shankarseth Road

Goan Institute Building and St. Francis Xavier Church

spot rows of old dilapidated buildings, many of them are chawls - the nucleus of the community living system in Mumbai. On closer observation, you might realise that tenants have been living there for several generations at rents fixed in the 1940s!

The demography of this road is equally interesting. Migrants from Konkan, Kutch, Kathiawar and Gujarat settled in Thakurdwar and the area along Prarthana Samaj (on Raja Rammohan Roy Road). The Maharashtrian Brahmins and Pathare Prabhus lived up to St. Teresa's Church (also called Portuguese Church). The Parsi community resided near the Hormusji Wadia Agiary and near Albless Baug (on Roy Road). The Christians lived either in the northern end of Girgaum, near Dhobi Talao or in Khotachiwadi.

It's interesting to see the manner in which migration from Goa began, in the late nineteenth century itself. Most migrants settled in tiny alleys and bylanes of Girgaum around St. Francis Xavier Church and St. Teresa's Church. In the vicinity sprung up several Christian enclaves like the area surrounding the Goan Institute Building and the nearby St. Francis Xavier Church. This building stands out for its different architectural style. Built of granite stone and arches, reminiscent of old government buildings in the Fort area, it invites curious looks from pedestrians. In its glory days, it must have been a hotbed of social activity, acting as the vanguard of the community in the area. Nearby, the St. Francis Xavier Lane off Shankarseth Road leads you to the St. Xavier's Church.

Many 'clubs' were also set up by people from Goa in this area. Some of the more popular ones were the Club Lusitano da Associacao Dramatica on Picket Road, Goa National Dramatic Company on Girgaum Road, the Indo-Portuguese Cricket Club of Bombay, the Instituto Luso-Indiano at Agiary Street and the Instituto de Sto. Antonio (the old Anglo-Portuguese School). Sadly, none of them remain today.

Majestic Cinema

If you are in Girgaum and wish to reach parts near Khotachiwadi, just tell your cab driver or bus conductor 'Majestic' and you are brought to the area without any hiccups. But, what or where is this area that carries this name? Well, Majestic was a famous cinema hall in the very heart of Girgaum that was demolished a few years ago and replaced by a commercial and shopping complex, with several commercial buildings mushrooming in its vicinity. Nonetheless, people still refer to the

place as 'Majestic'! Once upon a time, Majestic was one of the most popular cinemas to screen Marathi films. Hindi films were also a huge draw, though the hall largely catered to the large middle-class Marathi-speaking population of Girgaum, Khetwadi and Dhobi Talao.

Tucked away in the St. Francis Xavier's Lane is the St. Francis Xavier's Church, established in 1870. Beside it, is the St. Sebastian School, set up in the 1920s
▼

*Khotachiwadi is a quaint village off
Sir J. Shankarseth Road. A few paces inside the
lane and you spot a chapel that was built in 1899.
The village is home to the Girgaum Catholic Club.
A board outside the club's premises proudly
mentions "Members Only"*

Interestingly, Majestic theatre has an envious date with Hindi film history. On 11 March 1931, *Alam Ara*, the first full length, locally-produced talkie film, was released at the Majestic Cinema. It was produced under the banner of the Imperial Film Company that was owned by noted Parsi Ardeshir Irani and his silent partner, Abdul Ali Yusuf Bhai. Though the film was partly made in sound, it created a tremendous impact at the box office. The public response at Majestic was simply overwhelming. Another first is associated with the cinema and this film. *Alam Ara*, also called 'The Light Of The World,' had a star cast of the time featuring Master Vithal, Zubeida, Prithvi Raj, Jillo Bai, Yaqub, Jagdish

Sethi and W.M. Khan.

Khotachiwadi

In the heart of Girgaum, off J. Shankarseth Road lies an urban village, a forgotten Portuguese pocket lost among the din and bustle of its surroundings. Here, the original plan of the village remains intact, almost as if time forgot to catch up with this settlement. The typical blue street nameplate says Khotachiwadi. You follow the instructions and walk into another world altogether. Khotachiwadi is still home to one of the largest concentrations of the Catholic community in south Mumbai. Narrow pathways, crucifixes at lane junctions and the odd chapel is part of the landscape.

Centuries ago, Girgaum was a colony of land tillers, a plantation land filled with palms and blessed with a tropical vegetation. With the demolition of the Fort in the 1800s, the population from the area moved towards the native town. The ruling East India Company ordered that the land should be divided beyond the fort to develop its resources and hence most of the land here was leased to individual cultivators. Khotachiwadi was assigned to Dadoba Waman Khot, a land revenue officer. He collected the produce of the land given on lease. Initially, the area was predominantly occupied by the Hindu community. He later sold these plots to his East Indian Christian friends in the area. These East Indians built their charming bungalows on this patch of land in Girgaum and in time, it appeared that this village has escaped the pressures of a burgeoning metropolis. The pattern and style of the houses are unique and representative of nineteenth century structures. Most of the early residents were fisherfolk by profession. In time, many of them

CULINARY MUSINGS

One eatery that comes to the mind while in Khotachiwadi is **Anantashram**. While the restaurant may appear basic to the fussy, it's the seafood menu that will make you forget your surroundings! Its clientele includes some of the city's most illustrious figures. Interestingly, members of the management here are also seen doubling up as waiters in their vests and pajamas!

47G, Khotachiwadi is another well-known address within the area that receives a regular set of visitors from the Page three circuit. This quaint nook tucked away in sleepy Girgaum is the home of James Ferreira Couture, where the famous Goan designer and couturier has set up his signature store.

The chapel at the entrance of Khotachiwadi was built in 1899
▼

moved to the other Christian enclaves of Cavel, Mazagaon and further southward, in Bandra. Some of the most distinct features include shaded porches, timber and cast-iron balconies with intricate carvings, wooden staircases and roofs lined with Mangalore tiles. A peep into these homes and you see some wonderfully carved mahogany and teak furniture reminiscent of homes in Old Goa, grand European paintings and artwork showcased in carved frames as well as pianos with wooden finishes. Strains of Portuguese songs fill the air from gramophone players...each moment is worth every extra mile of this extended stopover along the walk. In 1880, it was officially named Khotachiwadi by the Bombay Municipal Corporation. In fact, since the 1930s, many villas and ancestral bungalows have been demolished or sold out to make room for modern structures. Khotachiwadi began to lose its unique fabric and appearance and is fighting a desperate war against land sharks to retain its identity.

Even today, this heritage site is fast losing its identity in the midst of rampant industrialisation that has not spared this tiny settlement. What remains are a handful of these bungalows and villas from a different time. The overall appearance of the architecture is vernacular and traditional with some glimpse of an expected Portuguese influence.

St. Teresa's Church

St. Teresa's Church, (also called the Portuguese church) and school is an important landmark at Girgaum. The Christian population from the surrounding locality (including Khotachiwadi) patronise the church. This church stands at the exact junction of Sir J. Shankarseth Road and Rammohan Roy Road and has been a mute spectator to the slow transformation of Girgaum. Its striking white-and-brick red structure greets the visitor at this crowded road junction.

Magistrate Building on Raja Rammohan Roy Road

DETOUR:

(Raja Rammohan Roy Road) Central Plaza cinema - Albless Baug - Prarthana Samaj - Sir Hurkisondas Hospital - Parsi Agiary - Magistrate's Building - Centenary Methodist Episcopal Church

At the road junction, near the Gordhandas Building, where Shankarseth Road meets Raja Rammohan Road, take a detour into Roy Road for a wider scan of the city's older parts. Take a left turn here and start off with the Central Plaza Cinema. This cinema, along with Majestic, screened Marathi films and was a favourite among the Marathi-speaking population of Girgaum and its surroundings. In January 1998, the sixty-year-old cinema at Girgaum caught fire, which completely destroyed the hall and foyer. Its new and improved version has stopped screening Marathi movies and seems to have lost a sizeable amount of the faithful local population in the process. Perhaps, a bit of history too.

A few paces ahead and the sprawling compound of the Albless Baug meets the eye.

Hurkisondas Nurottamdas Hospital on Raja Rammohan Roy Road

The area around this Baug is home to the Parsi population who settled here in the mid 1800s when efforts were underway to decongest the Fort area. Albless Baug was constructed in 1868 by the sons of a Parsi trader who did business with China. He was known as Edalji Framji 'Albless.' Interestingly, he earned the title 'Albless' because he always greeted everyone with a warm 'God Bless You All'!

Once you reach Albless Baug, take a U-turn back to the junction and walk further ahead along Roy Road till you sight the Prarthana Samaj. This organisation was started in Bombay and was inspired by the Brahmo Samaj but is milder and less radical in its principles. Social reform is its driving force, with issues like the abandonment of caste, widow-remarriage, female education, and the abolition of child-marriage as its core areas of work. Two secret societies preceded the Prarthana Samaj - the Gupta Sabha, and later,

in 1849, the Paramahamsa Sabha established by Ram Balkrishna Jaykar and others. The believers who held on to their convictions became the founders of the Prarthana Samaj in Bombay in 1867, mostly comprising of educated Indians from the city, led by Dr Atmaram Pandurang (1823-1898), a close friend of Dr. Wilson, founder of Wilson College, in 1835. Their own building was erected in 1874 at Girgaum on Dr. Rammohan Roy Road.

Just as you begin to soak in the charm of these old treasures, you spot skyscrapers that jerk you back to the realities of modern Mumbai, as tall as twelve floors on sites where once three or four-storeyed buildings stood. The famous cloth store - Babubhai Jagjivandas - is also located in Prarthana Samaj, a famous landmark in the area from the early 1980s.

A little further ahead along Rammohan Roy Road and you spot the Sir Hurkisondas Nurrotumdas Hospital that stands near the Girgaum Magistrate's Court. For decades together, this hospital has been treating the needs of the middle and lower class populace in the area. The hospital was established in 1925 by Sir Hurkisondas Nurrotumdas. Initially, it was a mere one-storey structure with forty beds. Half of them were free of cost, keeping in mind the charitable objective of Sir Nurrotumdas. In December 1997, a memorandum of understanding was signed between Sir Hurkisondas Nurrotumdas Hospital trust and Reliance Industries for a joint trusteeship. Reliance made a substantial contribution to upgrade the Sir Hurkisondas Nurrotumdas Hospital. Today, the hospital has undergone extensions from its original structure, including an adjacent plot of land and a twenty-one-storey complex with an exclusive basement car park facility.

Next in line is an age-old Parsi Agiary dating back to 1858. So high are the walls surrounding its compound that one barely manages to catch a glimpse of this fire temple. The structure is in good condition and is visited by faithful from the Girgaum vicinity, Charni Road and Grant Road. There is a most interesting building called Kapol Niwas nearby, which will capture your attention as it is an extremely narrow building in width.

The final stopover of the detour is the Centenary Methodist Gujarati Central Church, also called the Episcopal Church at the junction where Shaukat Ali Road meets with the Rammohan Roy Road. This church is frequented by a small Indian Christian congregation belonging to the Church of North India. An imposing gate greets the visitor to the church, forgotten among the bustle and din of this crowded road. The architecture is mostly vernacular. Interestingly, a board outside this church mentioning the timings for daily service is written in English and, surprise, surprise - Gujarati!

Once you return from this longish detour, take a U-turn back through Rammohan Roy Road till you return to the junction where this road rejoins with the Sir J. Shankarseth Road near the Voice of India Restaurant. Keep walking further down Shankarseth Road till you sight the dilapidated Royal Opera House to your left.

Royal Opera House

Situated on New Queen's Road, the grand Royal Opera House was planned in 1908 by J.F. Karaka with Maurice Bandmann, theatrical manager from Calcutta. By 1917, the Opera House began showing films and in 1925, the entire theatre was rented by the famous Pathe Cinema group. From 1929-32, it was leased to various Indian theatrical concerns including the Parsi Dramatic Company. Leading actors of the time like Bal Gandharva, Manji Khan, Bapu Pendharkar, Jaddanbai, Siddeshwari Bai and Nissar Hussain performed here. The stage theatre was converted in 1911 to show

Royal Opera House
▼

It's brisk business throughtout the year
at Zaveri Bazaar

imported feature films. This trend continued for decades together until the theatre began to run out of owners and its upkeep degraded. Gradually, this grand structure began to fade from public memory and lies abandoned today. As one walks past this crumbling landmark, it's almost unthinkable to imagine it as a spectacular building, filled with the rich and famous applauding a stellar performance from a travelling theatre company! Till today, the area and its surroundings are still referred to as 'Opera House'.

Zaveri Bazaar

Once you are done gazing at the forgotten glory of the Opera House, walk in the direction of Charni Road railway station till you are witness to a sea of activity, of a different kind. Here's a completely new experience altogether, a gold rush this side of the Great West! Rows of jewellery shops, glittering in the afternoon sun, from its huge glass window displays will lure the visitor. The ultimate paradise for jewellery lovers, Zaveri Bazaar can blur the senses with its sheer range on offer! With rows of jewellery stores and brands jostling for space, this street is the final stop for jewellery shopping in the city. The flagship store of this bazaar is Tribhovandas Bhimji Zaveri, or simply 'TBZ'. Tribhovandas began his tiny business when the British Raj was at the peak of its powers in India, in the year 1864. He had big dreams to set up a flourishing gold business by starting a showroom in the heart of the Indian jewellery market. His perseverance paid off and today TBZ is more than just another brand name in the gold and jewellery business. Several branches of TBZ have opened all over India. Its headquarters showroom at Zaveri Bazar is rated as one of the largest showrooms of its kind in Asia. The showroom, which is magnificent and opulent, is spread over five palatial floors.

౸౬

Bandra Revisited: Sights and Sounds of a Famous Suburb

(Bandra Railway Station - Hill Road - Castella De Aguado)

The history of this once-sleepy village on the outskirts of the island city, situated on one of the Salsette islands goes back to the 1500s. Portuguese traveller, Faria Sousa first mentioned Bandra in 1505 as a coastal town in Konkan. By 1507, the Portuguese made this prosperous seaside village one of their important posts. Records suggest that the Portuguese may have burned down most of the township by 1532. A century later, the Portuguese built a fort called the Castella de Aguado. This, along with the nearby chapel became the nucleus of the village that dotted the coast along the Arabian Sea. Today, they remain invaluable treasures that have stood the test of time.

The township earned further attention when the British East India Company occupied it in 1774 and later, when the Mahim Causeway was built as a link between Salsette islands and the main Bombay island. In the late 1860s, Bandra witnessed an exodus, with thousands fleeing the mainland when the plague epidemic ravaged the city. Even in the mid-1900s, most of the rich population invariably owned a quaint villa or beach house in Bandra. Concrete jungles may have not even spared this quaint suburb, yet it was and still remains a much-preferred location. No wonder, few argue that the title —'The Queen of the Suburbs'—shouldn't be conferred on any other locality!

APPROXIMATE DISTANCE
4 kilometres

PLACES OF INTEREST
❖ Bandra Railway Station

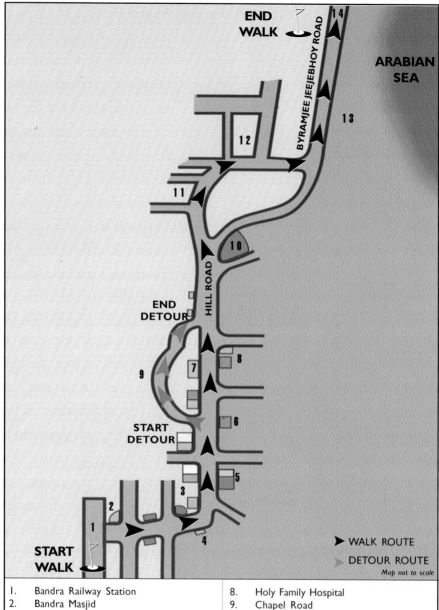

END
WALK

ARABIAN
SEA

BYRAMJEE JEEJEBHOY ROAD

14

13

12

11

10

HILL ROAD

END
DETOUR

9

7

8

6

START
DETOUR

5

3

2

4

1

START
WALK

► WALK ROUTE

► DETOUR ROUTE

Map not to scale

1.	Bandra Railway Station	8.	Holy Family Hospital
2.	Bandra Masjid	9.	Chapel Road
3.	Lucky Restaurant	10.	St. Andrew's Church
4.	Bandra Police Station	11.	Mehboob Studio
5.	Elco Arcade	12.	Mount Mary's
6.	St. Joseph's Convent		Church
7.	St. Stanislaus High School and	13.	Bandstand
	St. Peter's Church	14.	Bandra Fort

- ❖ Masjid and surrounding street market
- ❖ Lucky Restaurant
- ❖ Bandra Police Station
- ❖ Parsi Agiary on Hill Road
- ❖ Hill Road
- ❖ St. Joseph's Convent
- ❖ **DETOUR:** Chapel Road
- ❖ St. Stanislaus High School and
  St. Peter's Church
- ❖ Holy Family Hospital
- ❖ Hersche Bakery, American Express
  Cleaners and Bakery and
  A-1 Stores & Bakery
- ❖ St. Andrew's Church
- ❖ Mehboob Studio
- ❖ Mount Mary's Church
- ❖ Bandstand and adjoining areas
- ❖ Bandra Fort

THE WALK

This walk takes you through some of the most historic and memorable roads, bylanes and landmarks that give Bandra its unique flavour and charm.

Bandra Railway Station

The Bombay Baroda & Central India Railway expanded its route to connect the main Bombay island with its neighbouring islands, namely Salsette. The idyllic township of Bandra was situated in the south-west part of Salsette. Here, the Mithi river meets with a broad tidal creek, popularly known (even till today) as Mahim Creek, which separated Bandra from Mahim in the Bombay island. From 1845, a causeway was built to bridge the creek for vehicular traffic. Likewise, in 1867, the BB&CI Railway - now the Western Railway - built a rail-bridge over the creek for rail traffic. With its mix of vernacular and Gothic architecture, the Bandra railway station is listed as a Grade-I heritage structure. The

DID YOU KNOW?

Between 1505 and 1688, historians have referred to **Bandra** as Bandor, Bandera, Bandara, while ancient Marathi documents mention Vandra. This suburb with abundant greenery and residential neighbourhoods even had sandy beaches, tiny hills and little villages, separated by rice fields and vegetable gardens. The Portuguese decided to adopt the name Bandora. By 1894, the BB&CI Railway changed the name to Bandra. It was in April 1867, with the introduction of the rail service, that Bandra gradually underwent a change as people from overcrowded areas of the island city invaded its sleepy environs. The Bandra Municipality was formed in 1876; this led to bus services for Bandra, town planning schemes, educational institutions, building of agiarys (fire temples), temples, churches and mosques, hospitals and shopping centres at a rapid pace.

original Mangalore-tiled roofing of the main structure is intact, so are the flagpoles, the wooden architecture as well as its outer façade. The landscape around Bandra railway station may have changed but this heritage structure remains an apt reminder of the suburb's glorious past.

Bandra Masjid and the surrounding street market

Step out of the railway station and calls of the muezzin from the nearby Bandra mosque will greet you. This place of worship is hard to miss, even as devotees jostle for room to offer their namaz amidst the bustle outside the railway station in this highly congested locality.

You proceed further, and the aroma from the local street food market is irresistible. Not for the calorie conscious and delicate-tongued, these restaurants can lure the foodie with their sumptuous fare, ranging from the baida paratha (a paratha stuffed with minced meat and egg), beef kebabs, boti kebabs and the ever-popular tandoori chicken. These restaurants have constituted the street market for decades together and are integral to this chaotic side of Bandra. Walk on and you see aquarium shops, estate agents and even an undertaker. So much for variety! The 'caramel custered' (spellings on these menus will amuse the first timer!) and kulfi falooda available in one of the 'family' restaurants nearby are simply divine. The customer is caught completely unawares

while searching for a wash basin. Instead, a bearer will come to your table with brass water jug, hand basin and towel in tow, to actually wash your hands, maharaja style! This is truly living life king-size!

Further ahead, you spot a line of dealers selling second-hand, garish furniture, in semi-usable state and, for the most part, a complete eyesore. On the opposite side are rows of shops selling 'imported' goods - from 'Ray Ben' eyewear to 'Lotoo' sportswear!

Lucky Restaurant

It's been fifty years and more, yet the popularity of this prominent landmark in Bandra seems to be growing by leaps and bounds. If you have a weakness for tandoori

Above: The Bandra mosque and
its adjoining area
Left: Bandra Railway Station

cuisine and biryani, this could be your
ultimate food destination in Bandra. People
swear by its chicken biryani, reshmi kebabs,
mutton delicacies and faloodas. The service
is swift, the interiors non-fussy but
what's served from that sumptuous menu is
what matters the most. Walk in at any
time of the day and chances of getting a
free table is quite uncertain. Evolving from a
small-time restaurateur, Lucky has now
branched out, having set up a full-fledged
hotel, bakery and fast-food outlet as well as
an electronics store.

Bandra Police Station

Established in 1940, this building, housing
the Deputy Commissioner's Office, stands
as the suburb's upright caretaker, maintaining
law and order. The granite exterior looks
bright with a fresh coat of yellow paint and
its Mangalore-tiled roof makes it a charming

addition to the landscape. With its general
air of hectic activity, the wooden building's
staircases and balconies, leafy exteriors
certainly impress the first-timer; you almost
forget its actual purpose of existence!

Parsi Agiary

The Panthaki Tata Agiary is a small fire
temple, hidden away from the public gaze
mainly due to its high walls. It stands at a
juncture just before you enter the chaos and
activity that Hill Road is so famously known
for. The Parsi population around this part of
Bandra frequents this place of worship. A tiny
store catering to the needs of the community
is situated alongside.

Hill Road

Hill Road, along with Linking Road,
remains suburban Mumbai's first real fashion
street. For decades, suburbanites flocked here
to shop at the many department and shopping
centres, coupled with rows of roadside
vendors and self-styled fashion boutiques.

Interestingly, this road was built way back in 1854. Throughout this stretch, amidst the bustle and din, images of the older Bandra play hide and seek. A sneak peak into any of the countless lanes and alleys will give the first-timer an insightful glimpse, a slice of old Goa sitting pretty in the very heart of commercial Bandra.

You simply cannot miss Elco Arcade, which came up sometime in the 1970s. Surrounded by many more new stalls and swish boutiques, together they represent one of the most vibrant shopping districts of the city. Nothing beats window-shopping along this crowded turf. Customers haggling with roadside hawkers and vendors for a better price is a common sight. Two of the older establishments on Hill Road are Hilton and Parison. These are two of the most recognisable 'fashion' stores that go back to the time when Hill Road became the revered fashion Mecca for shopaholics all over the city. Situated a stone's throw from each other, they were the final statements in fashion and style for the average Bandraite, until the newer, bolder and trendier boutiques as well as mall-mania swept the suburb. Decades have passed yet they have managed to hold their own. Come Christmas or Easter and these two stores are flooded by their faithful clientele from Bandra and beyond who prefer their conservative, albeit slightly predictable styles to the more adventurous cuts on display elsewhere.

A stroll further down will seem like an endless flash of neon signs, trendy boutiques, whizzing traffic, crowds - typical of the character of this bustling suburb, until the wee hours of the night. Some of the other older businesses are the Bata Shoe Store, JJ Dias & Sons Men's Wear, established in 1930, (one of

Above: Bandra Police Station

Right : The famous panipuriwala is an important occupant of Elco Arcade

St. Joseph's Convent

the oldest tailors in Bandra) and Cheap Jack (known for their knick-knacks, decorations, novelties for decades together). In fact, if residents are to be believed, the Bata store here is touted to be one of the oldest in the suburbs. The nearby Bandra Medical Stores is another old-timer, known to stock some of the most rare medicines.

Cheap Jack: The famous gift shop remains a favourite among Bandraites

St. Joseph's Convent

Walk a few paces and you spot a brick-coloured structure to your right - St. Joseph's Convent. This convent school is probably one of the earliest to be established in the suburbs, in 1863. The original structure, including the school building and the chapel, has been renovated. According to historians and old timers in the suburb, the site of the ancient village of Partharwar, now extinct, has been occupied by St. Joseph's Convent. The day

school, boarding and orphanage are run by the Order of the Daughters of the Cross, founded in 1855 in Liege, Belgium. One step into these serene surroundings and you notice the carefully tended gardens and pathways, coloured with button roses and multi-coloured bougainvillea. Its chapel is another beautiful construction that deserves a stopover.

DETOUR: Chapel Road

Take a short detour into Chapel Road for a peep into old Portuguese styled bungalows and cottages. A Goan Christian enclave, the area is a heritage site in itself as since most of these homes have remained intact since the 1930s and 1940s. But first, a little history about the evolution of the Bandra village, of which only few remnants survive. In 1695, the original area that comprised Bandra was divided into twenty-five settlements. A few of these are still around. Salgado is the modern-day Khar, Xelalim and Rajana have

A bungalow at the entrance to Chapel Road

become the Sherly-Rajan village, Cantawari is the Kantwadi area; Colario Grande is Koliwada, and Colario de Igreja is the modern-day Chimbai. What was known as the Bandra Village is the area contained in the triangle between St. Andrew's, Mount Carmel and St. Peter's churches. The original village of Bandra is long gone. What remains are settlements that have sprung up between the older ones.

Chapel Road is one such remnant of old Bandra, replete with quaint old homes; crosses at every lane junction greet you. As you walk down Chapel Road, the 'Fresh' Pork Market is what you first spot. Every evening and throughout Sundays, crowds swarm this place. Some of the oldest and most sought after caterers in Bandra—Lucky Star and Jeff—are located here. Notice how each block carries a number plate. A huge, wooden cross stands at the entrance as the road splinters into several lanes. Most homes appear to have been modelled on a Portuguese layout. Sloping roofs, external wooden staircases, verandahs, narrow balconies and tiny gardens can be spotted. Many of these homes date back to over fifty years and are either one or two-storeyed villas.

In fact, you even spot interesting names for these homes, like Baptista House or Anaclete House and there's even Queen Victoria's face engraved on the balcony railings of one home! Crosses can be seen at every street corner and you begin to lose count after crossing thirty-five. Goan jewellery stores and travel agents that lure you to Goa are scattered throughout this stretch. Unfortunately, many of the older homes have been razed and in their place, concrete buildings have risen.

St. Stanislaus High School
▼

St. Stanislaus High School and St. Peter's Church

St. Stanislaus was the first English boys' school in Bandra and probably in suburban Mumbai, built in 1861. The Fathers and Brothers of the Society of Jesus started it as an orphanage. The Roman Catholic Diocese of Mumbai runs the school. Since its establishment, it has been in the forefront of education in the suburb. It continuously contributes towards nurturing talent in academics as well as producing some of the brightest sporting talent, especially in hockey and football. The school is a landmark of Bandra and holds a special place in the hearts of its citizens for the invaluable role it continues to play in its development. The adjoining St. Peter's Church is also situated in its premises. It was built in 1939. This large, impressive building has come a long way from being a temporary chapel of bamboo, thatched with coconut leaves, way back in 1879. Today, as one walks towards its entrance, numerous graves can be seen in its courtyard, with sun-dried flowerbeds and melted candles.

Proceed further down Hill Road and the road widens. The landscape is truly an interesting mix of the old and new. One and two-storeyed villas stand alongside striking-white luxury apartments, old businesses jostle for an extra inch of space, struggling for survival, even as their upmarket counterparts continue to nudge their way into their territories.

Holy Family Hospital

Another integral part of this suburb is the Holy Family Hospital. In 1978, His Eminence Cardinal Valerian Gracias, Archbishop of Bombay felt that the suburbs were in dire need of an affordable healthcare centre. With this concern, the Holy Family Hospital and Medical Research Centre was born. It was built to cater to the suburban populace, that comprised a vast and varied geographic, demographic, socio-economic and religious profile. The hospital offered economical treatment for those in a position to pay, and free medical care for the under-privileged. It began in 1985, as a 100-bed hospital and is today a 225-bed medical institution and research centre, under the care and trusteeship of the Ursuline Sisters of Mary Immaculate.

J. Hearsch & Co. Bakery, American Express Bakery and A-1 Stores & Bakery

Each of these stopovers are veritable institutions, especially to the old Bandraite. Tucked away from public gaze, near the Holy Family Hospital, is the famous Hearsch Bakery, known for its lip-smacking brownies, muffins, marzipan and pastries. Nearby is the American

St. Stanislaus was the first English boys' school in Bandra and probably in suburban Mumbai, built in 1861. The Fathers and Brothers of the Society of Jesus started it as an orphanage

A water fountain, dating back to 1894, erected just outside the boundary walls of St. Andrew's Church
▼

St. Andrew's Church

Express Bakery, another favourite for its oven-fresh breads, cakes and other baked goodies. The American Express Bakery is a tiny smoke-blackened bakery where the whiff of freshly baked bread pervades the air. Crowds can be seen swarming this nondescript place every evening for its legendary oven-fresh brun pao, baked bread and other goodies. Likewise, A-1 Stores & Bakery is renowned for their wafers for decades together. Morning hours witness huge crowds flocking these shops to grab the freshest, before they vanish off the counter.

St. Andrew's Church

Churches are more or less synonymous to this part of Bandra as one proceeds further on this walk. The St. Andrew's Church and the adjacent Apostolic Convent are pivotally situated at the end of Hill Road. St. Andrew's Church is the oldest standing structure in Bandra. It was built in 1575 when the Portuguese missionary Father Manuel Gomes reached this village. This original structure was stucco-plastered and lightly embellished in the style of most Portuguese-Goan churches and was set in the middle of large burial grounds.

Till 1853, it was the only place where residents of Bandra could bury their dead. Old illustrations of the area show a large sloping roofed porch, added on in 1890. Today, the church and its surrounding have changed and more graves occupy the churchyard. Bandra historians stated that in May 1618, a huge storm occurred in the neighbourhood and twenty-five churches were damaged. In this storm, the roof of St. Andrew's Church flew off. This apart, the church has remained in good shape till today. In its yard a large cross was moved by a certain Father Francis D'mello and set on a pedestal in 1870.

Mehboob Studio

Instead of taking the road ahead to your right, towards Bandstand, opt for a left turn where you see a stretch of old residences down the road. The sea breeze plays hide and seek and the road narrows. Keep walking till this road reaches a bend, take the right and proceed past the famous Damien Interiors until it becomes a climb. Within a few paces, you instantly spot a huge gate on your right-hand side and that's the legendary Mehboob Studio.

Mehboob Studio was built in 1952 and soon became a landmark in this suburb. It witnessed the shooting of memorable films like *Mother India* that Mehboob Khan made immediately after completing the studio. Other great films that were made here include *Andaz, Roti, Aurat* and almost all of Dev Anand's films including *Hum Dono* and *Guide*. Mehboob Khan built this famous studio at a time when Mumbai was replete with film

The famous and historically significant cross placed inside the St. Andrew's Church premises

▼

DID YOU KNOW?

The seventeen-feet-high cross inside the **St. Andrew's Church** premises is one of the oldest crosses in the city. Noted city historian and authority on Bandra, Brinda Gaitonde, in her writings on Bandra explains that unlike most crosses that are made of at least two pieces of stone, this cross is carved out of a single block. Incidentally, this cross was commissioned for the Portuguese royal family and was brought from the College of St. Anne's, which was located where the BEST bus depot stands today. A fortified wall surrounded the College, which housed the colony. Sometime in the eighteenth century, the British, who controlled the area from Colaba to Mahim wanted to weaken the Portuguese influence in these parts and so blew up the fortification. The cross was rescued and reinstalled at St. Andrew's Church.

studios. His dream was to make a state-of-art studio at a good location. It was leased to other producers whenever Mehboob Khan was not shooting his films. No wonder Dev Anand made most of his films under the Navketan banner at these studios, except the last two or three. Unfortunately, a fire devastated these studios on 18 December 2000. The studio has never really reclaimed its days of glory since then and what remains is in dire need of repair.

Mount Mary's Church

Come 8 September, and the streets of Bandra are transformed into one, big, grand celebration. The grand old Basilica of Our

◄ *Mount Mary's Church*

Lady of the Mount is ready for the biggest event on its calendar to celebrate the annual feast. Commonly referred to as Mount Mary's Church, this striking Neo Gothic architectural building stands atop what was once part of a hillock and still occupies a prominent place along the Bandra skyline.

The church's humble origins date back to a small chapel in 1556, with the Portuguese constructing the Nossa Senhora de Monte church on the hilltop in 1640. This tiny place of worship was connected to the fort by a

The statue was kept at the Aguado and later moved to the St. Andrew's Church in the vicinity until the Mount Mary's Church was rebuilt in 1761, thanks to funding from parishioners

▲
One of the many bungalows in Bandra that date back to well over 50 years

►
Another imposing bungalow on Hill Road

narrow road to enable the garrison stationed inside the Aguado to attend services. The original chapel faced the wrath of the Maratha army in 1738. The famous statue of Mother Mary also went missing after the raid. According to local legend, the very same life-sized statue crafted in highly ornamental wood was actually recovered, six months later, by fishermen off the coast nearby! The statue was kept at the Aguado and later moved to the St. Andrew's Church in the vicinity until the Mount Mary's Church was rebuilt in 1761, thanks to funding from parishioners.

By then, the Portuguese had defeated the Marathas and this became a garrison church until the British got Bombay as part of the famous dowry of a Portuguese princess. Interestingly, the church gained popularity as a place to seek favours only in the nineteenth

century when a Parsi couple, Sir Jamshetjee Jeejeebhoy and Lady Jamshetjee, prayed for a child. The couple had lost all their daughters at infancy. He promised to build a causeway linking Bandra with Mahim, then separated by the sea, to ease the convenience of worshippers who came from other parts of Mumbai, if his new born daughter survived beyond the age of seven. They were blessed with a daughter and Jeejeebhoy not only fulfilled his promise by building a causeway but also the flight of steps that reach up to the mount from the eastern side.

The church was called Maulincha Dongar, which when translated meant 'Hill of the Mother' because the locals considered the Virgin Mother their mother goddess. A long flight of stone steps built on its eastern slope behind the church lead to the local market. With time, it grew to become the most important church in Salsette, and also the most revered. Centuries later, a new, enlarged and better-ventilated chapel was designed by Shapoorjee Chandabhoy and consecrated to

▲
Villa Vienna, now famously rechristened as Mannat, is the home of Bollywood superstar Shah Rukh Khan

Familiar, tiled-roof structures like these, en route to Bandstand, can be spotted all over this suburb
▼

the public on 11 May 1902 by the Bishop of Daman. This new church was an architectural marvel of its time-made from the local Khandki and Porbander stone, 110 feet long and 38 feet wide. Its inner gallery ran on three sides, including two new towers, each measuring eighty feet in height.

Thus a tradition was established which continues to this day. During the Fair, devotees congregate at the church and offer wax candles to seek favours through Mother Mary. The annual feast to celebrate Mary's birthday is also accompanied by a Bandra fair, which draws crowds of revellers. It is believed that over a million devotees visit the church during the annual ten-day festival. Across the church is a set of two flights of stairs that reach up to another spot to offer prayers. It gives a breathtaking view of the Arabian Sea. In 1954, Pope Pius XII gave it the status of a Minor Basilica, which received its most honoured visitor when Pope Paul VI visited it in 1964 during his trip to India.

Bandra's famous Khoja Florists located towards the end of Hill Road where it reaches the seafront

▼

Bandstand and adjoining areas

After the uplifting experience at Mount Mary's, proceed towards Bandstand. Here, the landscape oscillates from historic to modern. Throughout this stretch, Mediterranean-styled residences set against clear skies can be spotted alongside several skyrises. As you walk towards land's end, you also spot quaint-sounding lanes like Kane Road and Bullock Road winding off from sight. The sea is now in full view as the promenade leads it all the way to the ruins of the fort. Thanks to efforts of local citizens' groups the sea-facing promenade has undergone a remarkable makeover. This pathway, with tiny manicured lawns, benches and a mini open-air amphitheatre is packed with walkers, joggers, or bystanders enjoying the gentle sea breeze. Along the bandstand frontage, by Byramjee Jeejeebhoy Road, the Parsi Sanatorium, the Khoja Sanatorium (now being reconstructed), Keki Manzil, Firdosh Manzil, Marine Mansion and Villa Vienna (now called Mannat, the present residence of Shah Rukh Khan) stand out among others. Old timers remind you how Bandstand earned its name

because of the bands that would play here for local residents. There was a time when this once-idyllic area was filled with families, especially during school vacations. Young and old would sit by the sea edge waiting for a good catch of fish, pack them in bottles and take them home!

Castella de Aguado (Bandra Fort)

Way past the promenade and rows of street food stalls and five-star hotels, a tiny clearing can be spotted. You've reached Land's End. Walk a few metres ahead and you manage to sight a few ruins of what was once the

◄

The surviving ruins of what was once known as the Castella de Aguado or the Bandra fort at Land's End, facing the Arabian Sea

A statue in black stone of a bull overlooking the rocky shore below, goes almost unnoticed at the Bandstand promenade
▼

Castella de Aguado. The island city was guarded by forts built by the conquerors of the time, and Portuguese forts dotted the landscape at several points along the coast. Bandra was home to one of them - Castella de Aguado. A few of its ruins still remain at Land's End. The Bandra fort dates back to the 1600s. The Castella was built as a pivotal structure that overlooked the Arabian Sea. It is still possible to climb up and sit among the ruins and imagine what it must have been like for the Portuguese soldier, over 400 years ago, alone in an alien, tropical land, trying to hang on to a patch of valuable property for his King and country.

৪০৫৪